The *Secret* Sex Lives of the Romans

Harper Calloway

BELLANOVA

MELBOURNE · SOFIA · BERLIN

Copyright © 2023 by Harper Calloway

The Secret Sex Lives of the Romans
HARDCOVER
ISBN: 978-619-264-164-1
Imprint: Bellanova Books

All rights reserved. No part of this book may be reproduced in any form by any electronic or mechanical means including photocopying, recording, or information storage and retrieval without permission in writing from the author.

Contents

Introduction 4
Roman Sexuality: An Overview 7
The Roman Social Ladder 14
Sexual Imagery in Roman Art and Architecture 20
The Art of Seduction 28
Roman Love Stories and Myths 34
Marriage, Adultery, and Divorce 43
The Brothels of Rome 52
Sexual Symbols 62
Gods, Goddesses, and Fertility Cults 69
Homosexuality in Ancient Rome 76
Pederasty and the Roman Elite 85
Roman Sex Education 91
Gender Roles and Stereotype 97
Sexual Taboos and Deviance 105
The Role of Sex in Roman Politics 114
Medical Knowledge and Sexual Health 120
The Decline of Roman Morality 129
The Lasting Impact of Roman Sexuality on Western Culture 135
Index 141
Glossary 144

Introduction

Welcome to a world of passion, intrigue, and ancient desires! The Roman Empire, with its breathtaking architectural wonders, rich cultural heritage, and captivating tales of power and conquest, has long been a subject of fascination for history buffs and casual readers alike. One aspect of Roman society that has often been whispered about, yet rarely explored in detail, is the intimate realm of Roman sexuality. In this book, we're going to take a lighthearted journey into the secret sex lives of the Romans, uncovering the many surprising ways in which they experienced, understood, and expressed their desires, passions, and relationships.

As we set out on this exciting adventure, it's important to recognize that Roman sexuality was deeply intertwined with various aspects of Roman culture, society, and politics. Unlike our modern, Western notion of sexuality as a private matter, in ancient Rome, sex was a public affair, reflecting and reinforcing the power dynamics and social hierarchies that defined Roman life. This doesn't mean the Romans didn't have private and intimate experiences of love and desire. It simply means that these experiences were shaped by a complex web of social, cultural, and political factors that characterized the Roman world.

On our journey through the secret sex lives of the Romans, we'll encounter a wide array of sexual practices, beliefs, and attitudes. Some may seem familiar and relatable to modern readers, while others may appear exotic, strange, or even shocking. It's important to approach these topics with an open mind and a healthy dose of curiosity, recognizing that the Romans lived in a very different time and place, with different values, norms, and expectations. By doing so, we can gain a deeper understanding of the many dimensions of Roman sexuality and its lasting impact on Western culture and society.

In Chapter 1, we'll provide a broad overview of the main themes and issues that we'll explore in the subsequent chapters of this book. We'll examine the various factors that shaped Roman sexuality, such as the influence of Greek culture, the role of Roman law and social norms, and the impact of religion and mythology. We'll also discuss how Roman sexuality differed from our modern understanding, highlighting the unique features and characteristics of Roman sexual culture.

Throughout the following chapters, we'll delve deeper into specific aspects of Roman sexuality, exploring topics like the role of sex in Roman politics and power dynamics, the diverse forms of Roman sexual relationships, and the portrayal of sex in Roman art, literature, and popular culture. We'll also examine the ways in which Roman attitudes toward sex and morality evolved over time, reflecting broader social, cultural, and historical transformations.

By exploring the rich and complex tapestry of Roman sexuality, we'll uncover the many diverse and often surprising ways in which the Romans experienced, understood, and expressed their desires, passions, and relationships. As we do so, we'll gain valuable insights into the history of human sexuality and relationships, as well as the ways in which sex and morality have been constructed, negotiated, and transformed across different cultures and historical periods.

Roman Sexuality: An Overview

As we embark on our journey into the secret sex lives of the Romans, it's important to start with a broad understanding of the key themes and issues that shaped Roman sexuality. In this chapter, we'll explore the various factors that influenced Roman sexual culture, including the role of Greek culture, the impact of Roman law and social norms, and the significance of religion and mythology. We'll also discuss the unique features and characteristics that set Roman sexuality apart from our modern understanding.

The Greek Connection: Eros meets Amor

One of the most significant influences on Roman sexuality was Greek culture, which was highly respected and admired by the Romans. As the Romans conquered the Greek-speaking territories and absorbed much of their culture, they also adopted and adapted many of their ideas and practices related to sex and relationships.

The Greek concept of Eros, the god of love and desire, was embraced by the Romans, who transformed him into their own deity, Cupid (also known as Amor). The Greeks celebrated Eros as a force that could inspire both pleasure and pain, love and madness. The Romans, too, acknowledged the power and unpredictability of desire in their own art, literature, and mythology.

In addition to the influence of Greek mythology, the Romans were also exposed to Greek philosophy and the works of famous Greek writers, such as Sappho, Plato, and Aristophanes. These works often explored themes of love, desire, and sexuality, providing the Romans with a rich source of inspiration and ideas to draw from.

Sexual Double Standards: Roman Law and Social Norms

As in many societies throughout history, Roman society was characterized by a set of sexual double standards. Men were generally granted more sexual freedom and were expected to engage in extramarital affairs and relationships with both women and men. However, women, especially those of high social status, were expected to remain chaste and faithful to their husbands.

Roman law reflected these double standards, with adultery being a serious offense for a woman, but not for a man. A husband could even kill his wife if he caught her in the act of adultery, whereas a wife had no such legal recourse. This imbalance in sexual expectations and legal protection reinforced the patriarchal structure of Roman society, where men held most of the power and authority.

Despite these legal and social norms, Roman women were not entirely powerless. Some women, such as courtesans and actresses, were able to navigate the sexual double standards and use their sexuality to their advantage, gaining influence, wealth, and even political power.

Religion and Mythology: The Divine Dimension of Roman Sexuality

Religion and mythology played an essential role in Roman sexuality, with many gods and goddesses associated with love, desire, and fertility. Venus, the goddess of love and beauty, was the Roman counterpart of the Greek goddess Aphrodite. Mars, the god of war, was also linked to fertility and was often portrayed as the lover of Venus.

Roman mythology is filled with stories of love, lust, and desire, with gods and mortals engaging in various romantic and sexual escapades. These stories often served as cautionary tales, illustrating the power and unpredictability of desire, as well as the consequences of disobeying social norms and expectations.

The Romans also practiced various religious rituals and festivals that celebrated sexuality and fertility. The Lupercalia, for example, was a festival held in February, during which young men would run through the streets naked, whipping women with strips of goat hide to promote fertility. This raucous celebration was eventually replaced by the more subdued Christian festival of Valentine's Day.

Roman Sexuality in Daily Life

Roman society was highly stratified, with social class playing a significant role in shaping sexual experiences and relationships. Let's take a closer look at how Roman sexuality played out in the daily lives of people across different social classes.

Marriage and Family Dynamics

Roman marriages were typically arranged by the families involved, with a focus on political alliances, social standing, and financial considerations. Love and affection were not necessarily the driving forces behind these unions, but they could develop over time. In some cases, however, Roman marriages were simply a means to an end, and extramarital relationships were relatively common.

Despite the prevalence of extramarital affairs, the Romans placed a high value on familial loyalty and the sanctity of the home. The ideal Roman wife was expected to be loyal, virtuous, and devoted to her husband and family, overseeing the management of the household and the upbringing of the children.

Slavery and Sexuality

Slavery was an unfortunate reality in ancient Rome, and slaves were often subjected to sexual exploitation and abuse by their masters. Roman law viewed slaves as property, and owners were generally free to engage in sexual relationships with them, regardless of the slaves' consent. Some slaves were even purchased specifically for sexual purposes, working as prostitutes or personal concubines.

It's important to note that not all sexual relationships between slaves and their owners were exploitative or abusive. In some cases, genuine affection and even love could develop between them, resulting in manumission (the act of freeing a slave) and even marriage.

Homosexuality and Bisexuality

Roman society was relatively accepting of same-sex relationships, particularly between men. However, it's essential to understand that Roman attitudes toward homosexuality differed significantly from modern perspectives. The Romans didn't view sexuality in terms of fixed categories like "gay" or "straight." Instead, they focused on the roles and behaviors within sexual relationships, with an emphasis on the power dynamics between partners.

Roman men were expected to be dominant and assertive in their sexual encounters, regardless of the gender of their partner. Engaging in passive or submissive sexual roles was considered shameful for a Roman man, as it was associated with weakness and femininity.

For Roman women, same-sex relationships were less visible and less well-documented than those between men. However, evidence suggests that such relationships did exist, particularly among women of higher social status who had more freedom and independence.

Prostitution and the Sex Trade

Prostitution was a common and accepted part of Roman society, and sex workers could be found throughout the Roman Empire. Brothels were legal and regulated by the state, with prostitutes required to register with the government and pay taxes on their earnings.

Although prostitution was a legitimate occupation, it was associated with low social status and moral disrepute. Most prostitutes were slaves or former slaves, and their lives were often difficult and precarious. Despite these challenges, some sex workers managed to achieve financial success and social mobility, gaining influence and power through their relationships with wealthy and influential clients.

The Lasting Legacy of Roman Sexuality

As we've explored in this chapter, Roman sexuality was a complex and multifaceted phenomenon, shaped by a diverse array of cultural, social, and political factors. The Romans' attitudes and practices regarding sex and relationships provide a fascinating insight into their society and the broader history of human sexuality.

The legacy of Roman sexuality can still be seen in many aspects of Western culture today, from our fascination with love stories and romantic dramas to the ongoing debates surrounding sexual morality, gender roles, and LGBTQ+ rights. By examining the secret sex lives of the Romans, we can better understand our own sexual history and the ways in which our attitudes and beliefs about sex and relationships have evolved over time.

In the following chapters, we'll delve even deeper into the world of Roman sexuality, exploring topics such as the role of sex in Roman politics and power dynamics, the diverse forms of Roman sexual relationships, and the portrayal of sex in Roman art, literature, and popular culture. We'll also examine the ways in which Roman attitudes toward sex and morality evolved over time, reflecting broader social, cultural, and historical transformations.

As we continue our journey through the secret sex lives of the Romans, we'll gain valuable insights into the history of human sexuality and relationships, as well as the ways in which sex and morality have been constructed, negotiated, and transformed across different cultures and historical periods.

The Roman Social Ladder: Sex, Power, and Status

Sex and power have always been intimately linked, and ancient Rome was no exception. In this chapter, we'll explore the complex interplay between sex, power, and social status in Roman society, focusing on the ways in which sexual relationships were used to navigate and negotiate social hierarchies. From the extramarital affairs of emperors and senators to the secret liaisons of slaves and freedmen, we'll uncover the role of sex in the quest for power and influence in ancient Rome.

The Power of Patronage: Sexual Favors and Political Influence

In Roman society, the patronage system played a crucial role in maintaining social order and enabling upward mobility (Shelton, 1998). Wealthy and influential individuals, known as patrons, would provide financial support, legal assistance, and other forms of aid to their clients in exchange for loyalty, political support, and sometimes sexual favors.

In some cases, Roman patrons would use sex as a tool to manipulate and control their clients, offering or demanding sexual relationships as a means of securing loyalty and obedience. For example, the Roman satirist Juvenal wrote of wealthy women who would use their sexual allure to control their male clients, ensuring their continued support and influence (Juvenal, Satires, 6.45-58). Similarly, some male patrons would engage in sexual relationships with their male or female clients, using the promise of sex and social advancement to maintain control over their social networks.

Sex and Status: The Rules of Roman Relationships

In Roman society, sexual relationships were governed by a complex set of social norms and expectations, which varied according to the status of the individuals involved (Cantarella, 1992). As we've seen in the previous chapter, Roman men were generally granted more sexual freedom than women, and were expected to engage in extramarital affairs with both women and men.

However, not all sexual relationships were considered equal in the eyes of Roman society. For men, the key distinction was between the acceptable sexual partners, such as slaves, prostitutes, and lower-class women, and the "off-limits" partners, such as high-ranking women and other men's wives. Engaging in sexual relationships with the latter group could result in social scandal, legal penalties, and even violence, as Roman men were fiercely protective of their honor and reputation.

For Roman women, sexual behavior was more tightly constrained, with chastity and fidelity being highly valued virtues. A Roman woman who engaged in extramarital affairs or sexual relationships outside of her social class risked social disgrace, divorce, and even death at the hands of her husband or male relatives.

Extramarital Affairs: The Roman Elite and Sexual Scandal

Despite these social norms and expectations, Roman history is filled with stories of sexual scandal and intrigue among the elite. Emperors, senators, and other high-ranking individuals were notorious for their extramarital affairs and sexual exploits, which often involved lower-class women, slaves, and prostitutes.

For example, the emperor Augustus, who famously championed a moral reform program to restore traditional Roman values, was rumored to have engaged in numerous affairs with the wives of other men (Suetonius, Life of Augustus, 69). Likewise, the emperor Nero was said to have married a freedwoman named Acte, despite her low social status and the disapproval of the Roman elite (Tacitus, Annals, 13.12).

These stories of sexual scandal among the Roman elite reveal the complex relationship between sex, power, and social status in ancient Rome. While elite men were expected to uphold the ideals of Roman morality and virtue, they were also granted considerable sexual freedom and autonomy, allowing them to engage in a wide range of sexual relationships without fear of social reprisal or legal consequences.

The Sexual Dynamics of Slavery and Freedom

As mentioned earlier, slaves in ancient Rome were often subjected to sexual exploitation and abuse by their masters. Roman law viewed slaves as property, and their owners were free to use them for sexual purposes, often without regard for their consent or well-being.

However, some relationships between owners and slaves led to something more meaningful, including marriage. For example, the famous Roman playwright Terence, who was a freed slave, married the daughter of his former master, indicating that their relationship transcended the boundaries of social status and hierarchy (Suetonius, On Illustrious Men, 12).

Same-Sex Relationships and Social Status

As we've seen in the previous chapter, Roman society was relatively accepting of same-sex relationships, particularly between men. However, Roman attitudes toward homosexuality differed significantly from modern perspectives, focusing on the roles and behaviors within sexual relationships rather than the gender of the partners involved.

For Roman men, engaging in same-sex relationships with lower-status individuals, such as slaves or prostitutes, was considered socially acceptable and even prestigious, as it reinforced their dominant position in the social hierarchy (Williams, 2010). However, engaging in same-sex relationships with other elite men could be seen as a threat to one's social standing and reputation, as it blurred the lines between power and submission.

Roman women's same-sex relationships, on the other hand, were less visible and less well-documented than those between men. The poet Sappho, who lived in the 6th century BCE and wrote about love between women, has long been associated with female homoeroticism in the ancient world (Parker, 1993).

Conclusion: Sex, Power, and Social Mobility in Ancient Rome

In this chapter, we've explored the complex and fascinating relationship between sex, power, and social status in ancient Rome. From the extramarital affairs of emperors and senators to the sexual dynamics of slavery and freedom, Roman society was shaped and influenced by a diverse array of sexual relationships and power dynamics.

Sexual relationships in ancient Rome were not just about pleasure and desire, but also about power, influence, and social mobility. By engaging in sexual relationships with individuals of different social statuses, Roman men and women could navigate and negotiate the complex hierarchies and power structures of their society, using sex as a tool to secure their position and advance their interests.

References

Cantarella, E. (1992). Bisexuality in the Ancient World. Yale University Press.

Parker, H. (1993). Sappho and Her Social Context: Sense and Sensuality. Signs, 18(2), 269-290.

Shelton, J. (1998). As the Romans Did: A Sourcebook in Roman Social History. Oxford University Press.

Suetonius, Life of Augustus. Translated by J.C. Rolfe. Loeb Classical Library, 1913.

Suetonius, On Illustrious Men. Translated by J.C. Rolfe. Loeb Classical

Sexual Imagery in Roman Art and Architecture: Expressions of Desire and Power

Roman art and architecture are renowned for their grandiosity, beauty, and intricate designs. Among the various forms of artistic expression, sexual imagery played a prominent role in reflecting the values and attitudes of Roman society towards love, desire, and power. In this chapter, we will explore the presence of sexual imagery in Roman art and architecture, examining the various contexts in which it was employed and the messages it conveyed. We will delve into the fascinating world of Roman erotic art and its role in shaping the cultural identity of the ancient world.

Fertility and Prosperity: The Pompeian Frescoes

One of the most well-known examples of sexual imagery in Roman art can be found in the frescoes that adorned the walls of homes and public spaces in the ancient city of Pompeii (Clar, 1991). These erotic scenes, which often depicted acts of lovemaking, were not considered taboo or offensive by the Romans, but rather were seen as symbols of fertility, prosperity, and the natural cycles of life (Clar, 1991).

The famous frescoes of the House of the Vettii, for example, include a series of erotic scenes that were likely intended to convey a sense of abundance and good fortune (Clar, 1991). Similarly, the Villa of the Mysteries, another well-preserved Pompeian residence, features a series of frescoes that depict the initiation of a young woman into the mysteries of the cult of Dionysus, with scenes of lovemaking and fertility rites underscoring the theme of spiritual and physical transformation (Wik, 1995).

Power and Status: Erotic Art in the Roman Elite

Sexual imagery was not limited to the realm of domestic and religious art, but also played a role in the expression of power and status among the Roman elite. One example of this can be found in the Warren Cup, a silver drinking vessel dating from the 1st century CE, which depicts explicit scenes of male-male sexual encounters (Mey, 1998). The Warren Cup, now housed in the British Museum, is believed to have been a luxury item owned by a wealthy Roman patron, and its explicit imagery may have been intended to convey a sense of power and sophistication, as well as to provoke conversation and admiration among guests (Mey, 1998).

Similarly, the phallic symbols that were commonly used as decorative elements in Roman architecture, such as the numerous examples found in Pompeii, served as both symbols of fertility and protection and as expressions of power and dominance (Var, 1996). These symbols, often incorporated into the design of fountains, boundary stones, and other architectural elements, were meant to ward off evil spirits and bring good fortune, while also asserting the authority and status of the property owner (Var, 1996).

Divine Love and Desire: Cupid and Venus in Roman Art

The gods and goddesses of ancient Rome were often depicted in scenes of love and desire, reflecting the close association between the divine realm and human passions. Cupid, the god of love and desire, and Venus, the goddess of love, beauty, and fertility, were popular subjects in Roman art, appearing in a wide range of media, from frescoes and mosaics to statues and reliefs (Ric, 2003).

A notable example of the Roman depiction of divine love is the Capitoline Venus [pictured right], a marble statue that is a Roman copy of the Greek Aphrodite of Cnidus by Praxiteles. This sculpture, housed in the Capitoline Museums in Rome, captures the essence of beauty and sensuality that defined

Venus in the Roman imagination.

Another example can be found in the frescoes of the House of Venus Marina in Pompeii, which depict scenes of Cupid and Venus engaged in various acts of lovemaking (Clar, 1991). These images not only celebrate the pleasures of love and desire but also serve as a reminder of the divine origins of these powerful human emotions.

Subversive Erotica: The Satirical and the Political

Not all sexual imagery in Roman art was intended to convey a sense of beauty, power, or divine favor. Some artists used erotic themes to challenge societal norms, poke fun at the pretensions of the elite, or make political statements (Var, 1996). One such example is the collection of erotic poems known as the "Priapeia," which feature the god Priapus, a symbol of male fertility and sexual potency, engaging in a variety of humorous and often obscene scenarios (Ric, 2003).

Another example of subversive erotica in Roman art can be found in the so-called "Spintriae," small bronze tokens featuring explicit sexual images that were likely used as a form of currency in Roman brothels (Var, 1996). These tokens, which depict a wide range of sexual acts and positions, have been interpreted by some scholars as a form of satirical commentary on the excesses and decadence of Roman society (Var, 1996).

Spintria token showing fellatio between two men.

Conclusion: Expressions of Desire and Power in Roman Art and Architecture

The presence of sexual imagery in Roman art and architecture is a testament to the diverse and complex ways in which love, desire, and power were intertwined in the ancient world. From the beautiful frescoes of Pompeii that celebrated fertility and abundance to the scandalous exploits of the gods and goddesses, Roman artists drew upon a rich array of themes and motifs to explore the many facets of human sexuality.

Far from being mere titillation or obscenity, these images served as powerful expressions of cultural values, social hierarchies, and political dynamics, offering a window into the minds and hearts of the Romans who created and enjoyed them. As we continue to study and appreciate the legacy of Roman art, the sexual imagery that pervades it serves as a reminder of the enduring power of love and desire to shape and define human experience.

References

Clarke, J. R. (1991). The Houses of Roman Italy, 100 B.C.-A.D. 250: Ritual, Space, and Decoration. University of California Press.

Meyer, M. (1998). The Warren Cup. The British Museum.

Richardson, L., Jr. (2003). A Catalog of Identifiable Figure Painters of Ancient Pompeii, Herculaneum, and Stabiae. Johns Hopkins University Press.

Stewart, A. (1992). The Venus de Milo Revisited. In N. de Grummond & B. Ridgway (Eds.), From Pergamon to Sperlonga: Sculpture and Context. University of California Press.

Varner, E. R. (1996). Eroticism and the Body Politic. Johns Hopkins University Press.

Wikander, C. (1995). The Villa of the Mysteries: Pompeii's Most Famous House. Journal of Roman Archaeology, 8, 320-324.

The Art of Seduction: Roman Love Poetry

The ancient Romans had a passion for love and desire, and they knew how to express it through their art, literature, and poetry. In this chapter, we'll explore the world of Roman love poetry and erotica, delving into the works of famous poets such as Catullus, Ovid, and Propertius, as well as the more explicit and sensual depictions of love in Roman art and artifacts.

The Language of Love: Roman Love Poetry

Roman love poetry was a popular and influential genre, with poets such as Catullus, Ovid, and Propertius capturing the hearts and minds of their readers with their evocative descriptions of love, desire, and passion. These poets were masters of the art of seduction, using their words to entice, enchant, and enthrall their lovers and readers alike.

Catullus: Love, Lust, and Heartbreak

Catullus, one of the earliest and most famous Roman love poets, wrote intensely personal and passionate poems that expressed the full range of human emotions, from the heights of ecstatic love to the depths of bitter heartbreak (Skinner, 2003). His poetry was characterized by its vivid imagery, bold language, and often shocking subject matter, with Catullus unapologetically celebrating his love affairs and sexual encounters in explicit detail.

One of Catullus's most famous poems, "Carmen 5," is a passionate declaration of love for his mistress, Lesbia, whom scholars believe to be a pseudonym for the Roman noblewoman Clodia Metelli (Skinner, 2003). In this poem, Catullus urges Lesbia to seize the day and enjoy their love to the fullest, savoring each and every moment of passion and pleasure:

> "Let us live, my Lesbia, let us love,
> and let the rumors of stern old men
> count for only a penny.
> Suns can set and rise again;
> but once our brief light has set,
> there's one unending night for us to sleep through."
> (*Catullus, Carmen 5, lines 1-6, translated by Peter Green*)

Ovid: The Art of Love and Seduction

Ovid, another famous Roman love poet, is best known for his Ars Amatoria, or "The Art of Love," a witty and playful guide to love and seduction that offers practical advice and tips for both men and women on how to win the hearts and minds of their lovers (Ovid, Ars Amatoria). Ovid's work was both entertaining and controversial, with its frank discussions of sexuality and its subversive take on traditional Roman values and morals.

In the Ars Amatoria, Ovid offers a wealth of advice on topics such as how to dress, how to flirt, and how to win over a lover through gifts and compliments. For example, he advises men to be attentive and generous to their lovers, showering them with gifts and praise:

> "Give her gifts, gifts persuade even the gods: gifts,
> I warrant you, are what first made a way for love."
> (*Ovid, Ars Amatoria, Book 1, lines 237-238, translated by A. S. Kline*)

Propertius: Love, Elegy, and the Roman Mistress

Propertius, another prominent Roman love poet, is best known for his elegies, a series of tender and evocative love poems dedicated to his mistress, Cynthia (Propertius, Elegies). Like Catullus and Ovid, Propertius used his poetry to explore the complexities and contradictions of love and desire, celebrating the joys and sorrows of his passionate affair with Cynthia.

Propertius's elegies are characterized by their emotional intensity, vivid imagery, and deep sense of longing and loss. In one of his most famous poems, Propertius describes the agony of being separated from Cynthia, as he lies awake at night, tormented by thoughts of her:

"The whole night I lay sleepless on my bed,
anxious for Cynthia's return; the long hours passed,
and still I lay awake, staring into the darkness."
(*Propertius, Elegies, Book 1, Poem 3, lines 1-3,
translated by A. S. Kline*)

The Role of Sexuality in Roman Religion and Mythology

The Romans' fascination with sex and desire extended to their religious beliefs and mythological narratives. From the passionate love affairs of the gods to the erotic escapades of mythological heroes, Roman religion and mythology were rich with tales of love, lust, and seduction (Wiseman, 2004).

The Gods of Love: Cupid, Venus, and Mars

In Roman mythology, the gods of love played a prominent role, with Cupid, the god of desire, and Venus, the goddess of love and beauty, often featuring in tales of passion and romance. Cupid, also known as Amor or Eros in Greek mythology, was depicted as a mischievous, winged child who would shoot arrows at gods and mortals alike, causing them to fall hopelessly in love.

Venus, the mother of Cupid, was herself a symbol of love, desire, and female beauty. She was often portrayed in Roman art and literature as a seductive and alluring figure, with many of the most famous love stories in Roman mythology involving her passionate affairs and romantic escapades. One of the most well-known of these tales is the love affair between Venus and

Mars, the god of war, which symbolized the powerful and irresistible attraction between the forces of love and violence (Ovid, Metamorphoses, Book 4).

The Erotic Adventures of Mythological Heroes

Roman mythology also featured numerous stories of love, lust, and sexual adventure involving mythological heroes and heroines. One such example is the tale of the hero Hercules, who was renowned for his strength and virility and was said to have fathered countless children with various mortal and immortal lovers (Apollodorus, Library, 2.4.11).

Another famous mythological figure known for his sexual exploits was the poet Orpheus, who was said to have been so overcome with grief at the death of his beloved wife, Eurydice, that he descended into the underworld to bring her back to life (Ovid, Metamorphoses, Book 10). Orpheus's tragic love story was a popular theme in Roman art and literature, symbolizing the power of love to overcome even the most insurmountable obstacles.

Conclusion: The Enduring Legacy of Roman Love Poetry and Erotica

As we've seen in this chapter, the ancient Romans were passionate and expressive lovers, with a deep appreciation for the art of seduction and the many complexities and contradictions of love and desire. From the passionate verses of Catullus, Ovid, and Propertius to the sensual imagery of Roman art and the erotic tales of their gods and mythological heroes, the Romans left a rich and vibrant legacy of love, lust, and passion that continues to captivate and inspire us today.

In the next chapter we take a closer look at other ways in which the Romans expressed their sexuality through art.

References

Clarke, J. R. (1998). Looking at Lovemaking: Constructions of Sexuality in Roman Art, 100 B.C.–A.D. 250. University of California Press.

Clarke, J. R. (2007). Roman Sex: 100 B.C. to A.D. 250. Abrams.

Propertius, Elegies. Translated by A. S. Kline. Poetry in Translation, 2001.

Richlin, A. (1992). The Garden of Priapus: Sexuality and Aggression in Roman Humor. Yale University Press.

Skinner, M. B. (2003). Catullus in Verona: A Reading of the Elegiac Libellus, Poems 65-116. The Ohio State University Press.

Ovid, Ars Amatoria. Translated by A. S. Kline. Poetry in Translation, 2001.

Catullus, Carmen. Translated by Peter Green. University of California Press, 2005.

Wiseman, T. P. (2004). The Myths of Rome.

Roman Love Stories and Myths: Passion, Tragedy, and Triumph

Throughout history, love stories and myths have captivated the human imagination, offering tales of passion, tragedy, and triumph that resonate across cultures and generations. Ancient Rome was no exception, with a rich tapestry of romantic tales and mythical narratives that both reflected and shaped the Roman understanding of love, desire, and human relationships. In this chapter, we will delve into the world of Roman love stories and myths, exploring their themes, characters, and enduring appeal.

Cupid and Psyche: A Tale of Love and Transformation

One of the most enduring and enchanting love stories from Roman mythology is the tale of Cupid and Psyche, a narrative that combines elements of romance, adventure, and transformation to tell the story of a love that transcends mortal boundaries (Apu, 1989). This tale, recounted in "The Golden Ass" by the Roman writer Apuleius, tells of a beautiful mortal princess named Psyche who is envied by the goddess Venus for her beauty. In her jealousy, Venus sends her son Cupid, the god of love, to make Psyche fall in love with the most hideous creature on Earth (Apu, 1989).

However, Cupid accidentally pricks himself with one of his own arrows and falls deeply in love with Psyche. Instead of carrying out his mother's orders, Cupid takes Psyche to a hidden palace and marries her, but he insists that she must never look upon his face, as he is a god and she is a mortal (Apu, 1989). Psyche, driven by curiosity and the advice of her jealous sisters, ultimately disobeys Cupid's command and gazes upon his divine form, causing him to flee and abandon her.

In her quest to win back Cupid's love, Psyche undergoes a series of trials set by Venus, each more difficult and dangerous than the last (Apu, 1989). Through her determination, courage, and the help of various gods and magical creatures, Psyche ultimately completes the tasks, and she is granted immortality by Jupiter, allowing her to be reunited with her beloved Cupid. The tale of Cupid and Psyche serves as a powerful testament to the transformative power of love, and the lengths to which we are willing to go in its pursuit.

Dido and Aeneas: Love and Destiny in Virgil's Aeneid

Another captivating love story from ancient Rome is that of Dido, the queen of Carthage, and Aeneas, the Trojan hero and ancestor of the Romans, as recounted in Virgil's epic poem, the Aeneid (Virgil, 29-19 BCE). This tale, which unfolds against the backdrop of the founding of Rome and the destiny of the Roman people, explores the themes of love, fate, and the tragic consequences of defying the will of the gods.

After the fall of Troy, Aeneas and his followers set sail in search of a new home, as prophesied by the gods. Their journey leads them to Carthage, where they are welcomed by the beautiful and powerful Queen Dido (Virgil, 29-19 BCE). As Aeneas recounts the tragic tale of Troy's destruction, Dido falls deeply in love with him, and the two become entwined in a passionate affair. However, their love is not meant to last, as the gods have other plans for Aeneas and his people.

Jupiter, the king of the gods, sends a message to Aeneas, reminding him of his duty to fulfill his destiny and found a great new city (Rome) for his people (Virgil, 29-19 BCE). Aeneas, torn between his love for Dido and his divine duty, reluctantly decides to leave Carthage and continue his journey. Heartbroken and betrayed, Dido curses Aeneas and his descendants before taking her own life, setting the stage for the future enmity between Rome and Carthage (Virgil, 29-19 BCE).

The story of Dido and Aeneas is a poignant exploration of the tension between love and duty, and the heavy price that must sometimes be paid in the pursuit of a greater destiny. It also serves as a cautionary tale of the potential dangers of uncontrolled passion, and the need to temper our desires with a sense of responsibility and purpose.

Pyramus and Thisbe: Tragic Love in Ovid's Metamorphoses

Another tragic love story from Roman literature is the tale of Pyramus and Thisbe, recounted by the poet Ovid in his Metamorphoses (Ovid, 8 CE). This ancient tale, which predates even the Roman Empire, tells the story of two young lovers whose desire for one another leads to a tragic and untimely end.

Pyramus and Thisbe, a young man and woman from neighboring families, fall deeply in love but are forbidden to marry by their parents, who are embroiled in a bitter feud (Ovid, 8 CE). Undeterred by this obstacle, the two lovers devise a secret plan to meet at a nearby tomb under the cover of darkness. However, fate intervenes, and their plan goes horribly awry.

When Thisbe arrives at the tomb, she is frightened by a lioness and flees, leaving behind her veil (Ovid, 8 CE). The lioness, with her jaws stained from a recent kill, picks up the veil and tears it apart. Pyramus arrives at the scene to find the torn veil and assumes that Thisbe has been killed by the lioness. In his grief, he takes his own life, and when Thisbe returns to find her lover dead, she follows suit, plunging a dagger into her own heart (Ovid, 8 CE).

The tragic tale of Pyramus and Thisbe has been a source of inspiration for countless literary works throughout history, including Shakespeare's Romeo and Juliet, which shares many of the same themes and plot elements. The story serves as a powerful reminder of the destructive power of love when it is thwarted by fate and circumstance, and the enduring human desire for connection and intimacy in the face of seemingly insurmountable obstacles.

Hercules and Deianira: Love, Jealousy, and Betrayal

The love story of Hercules and Deianira, while not as well-known as some of the other tales in this chapter, is a fascinating exploration of the themes of love, jealousy, jealousy, and betrayal in the context of Greek and Roman mythology. Hercules, the legendary hero known for his immense strength and twelve labors, wins the heart of the beautiful Deianira after saving her from a river god who wishes to take her as his bride (Hesiod, 700 BCE). The two fall in love and marry, but their happiness is short-lived, as Hercules' infidelities and heroic exploits take their toll on their relationship.

During one of Hercules' adventures, he captures a centaur named Nessus, who offers to carry Deianira across a river to join her husband (Hesiod, 700 BCE). However, Nessus has ulterior motives and attempts to abduct Deianira. In response, Hercules shoots Nessus with a poisoned arrow. As he dies, Nessus tells Deianira that his blood, mixed with the poison from the arrow, will create a powerful love potion that will ensure Hercules' faithfulness (Hesiod, 700 BCE).

Deianira, blinded by her love for Hercules and her desire to save their marriage, uses the blood to create a potion and applies it to a robe for Hercules to wear. Tragically, the potion turns out to be a deadly poison, and Hercules is consumed by agonizing pain as the poison courses through his body (Hesiod, 700 BCE). Realizing her mistake, Deianira takes her own life in despair, leaving behind a legacy of love, jealousy, and betrayal that has echoed through the ages.

The story of Hercules and Deianira serves as a cautionary tale of the destructive power of jealousy and the unintended consequences of our actions, even when motivated by love. It also offers a sobering reminder of the vulnerability and fallibility of even the greatest heroes, and the human emotions that bind us all, regardless of our strength or status.

Orpheus and Eurydice: A Journey to the Underworld

The tale of Orpheus and Eurydice, another popular love story from Greek and Roman mythology, explores the themes of love, loss, and the limits of human endurance. Orpheus, a legendary musician and poet, falls deeply in love with the beautiful Eurydice, and the two are soon married (Ovid, 8 CE). However, their happiness is tragically cut short when Eurydice is bitten by a snake and dies, leaving Orpheus heartbroken and alone.

Unable to accept the loss of his beloved wife, Orpheus embarks on a perilous journey to the underworld to retrieve her, using the power of his music to charm the gods and win their favor (Ovid, 8 CE). Orpheus' music is so powerful that it moves Hades, the god of the underworld, to grant him permission to bring Eurydice back to the world of the living, under one condition: Orpheus must not look back at Eurydice until they have both safely emerged from the underworld.

As they make their way back to the surface, Orpheus is plagued by doubt and fear, and just as they are about to reach the exit, he can no longer resist the urge to look back at his wife (Ovid, 8 CE). In that moment, Eurydice is lost to him forever, and Orpheus is left to wander the world alone, mourning the loss of his love.

The story of Orpheus and Eurydice is a poignant exploration of love, loss, and the limits of human strength in the face of unimaginable sorrow. It acts as a powerful reminder of the enduring power of love and the lengths to which we are willing to go in its pursuit, even when faced with the most daunting of obstacles.

Romulus and Hersilia: Love, Abduction, and the Founding of Rome

The story of Romulus and Hersilia is intrinsically linked to the founding of Rome and offers a unique perspective on the role of love and desire in the creation of a great empire. Romulus, the legendary founder of Rome, and his followers found themselves in a precarious situation after establishing their new city: with a predominantly male population and a lack of female citizens, the long-term survival of Rome was at risk (Liv, 59 BCE - 17 CE).

To address this issue, Romulus and his men devised a plan to abduct women from the neighboring Sabine tribe during a festival held in honor of Neptune Equester, the god of horses and the sea (Liv, 59 BCE - 17 CE). During the festivities, the Romans seized the opportunity to abduct the Sabine women, including Hersilia, who would later become Romulus' wife.

The abduction of the Sabine women sparked a war between the Romans and the Sabines, which raged on until the women themselves intervened, led by Hersilia (Liv, 59 BCE - 17 CE). They bravely stepped between the warring factions, imploring their husbands and fathers to make peace and unite as one people. Moved by their courage and love, the Romans and Sabines agreed to end the conflict and formed a united society, with Hersilia and Romulus symbolizing the union between the two tribes.

The story of Romulus and Hersilia highlights the importance of love and desire in the founding of Rome and the formation of its unique cultural identity. It also serves as a reminder of the powerful role that women have played throughout history, not just as objects of desire, but as agents of change and catalysts for unity and peace.

Conclusion

The love stories and myths of ancient Rome offer a fascinating window into the Roman understanding of love, desire, and human relationships. From the passionate romance of Cupid and Psyche to the tragic tales of Dido and Aeneas or Pyramus and Thisbe, these stories reflect the full range of human emotions and experiences that have captivated the human imagination for millennia. By examining these tales, we gain a deeper understanding of the values, beliefs, and social norms that shaped Roman society and continue to influence our own ideas of love, desire, and the human condition.

References

Apu, L. (1989). The Golden Ass. Oxford University Press.

Hesiod. (700 BCE). Theogony.

Liv, T. (59 BCE - 17 CE). Ab Urbe Condita.

Ovid. (8 CE). Metamorphoses.

Virgil. (29-19 BCE). Aeneid.

Marriage, Adultery, and Divorce: Roman Relationships

When you think of Ancient Rome, you probably imagine majestic temples, powerful emperors, and fearsome gladiators. But what about the everyday lives of the Romans, particularly their love lives? This chapter delves into the world of Roman relationships, exploring the complexities of marriage, adultery, and divorce in a society that might surprise you with its moral flexibility (Potter, 2009).

Marriage: A Union of Convenience and Affection

The concept of marriage in Ancient Rome was quite different from our modern-day understanding. It was not so much a romantic union but rather a political and economic one, with the primary goal of producing legitimate heirs (Treggiari, 1991). Love was considered a delightful bonus, but it wasn't the main driving force behind tying the knot.

Roman Marriage: More Than Just Romance

In Roman society, marriage was often arranged by the couple's families, with an emphasis on social status, wealth, and the potential benefits that the union could bring to both parties (Bradley, 1991). As a result, affection and emotional compatibility were secondary considerations. However, this does not mean that love had no place in Roman marriages. Many couples grew to love each other deeply, as demonstrated by inscriptions and writings from the period (Williams, 2010).

Types of Roman Marriage: Cum Manu and Sine Manu

There were two main types of Roman marriage: cum manu (with the hand) and sine manu (without the hand). In a cum manu marriage, the wife was legally transferred from her father's authority to her husband's (Gardner, 1986). This type of marriage was more traditional and restrictive, requiring the wife to be obedient to her husband and placing her property under his control.

Sine manu, on the other hand, allowed the wife to remain under her father's authority, giving her more legal autonomy (Shelton, 1988). In these marriages, the wife maintained control over her property, and her husband had no legal power over her. As time went on, sine manu marriages became increasingly popular, reflecting a shift in societal attitudes towards women's rights (Treggiari, 1991).

Roman Wedding Ceremonies: A Celebration of Unity

Roman weddings were lavish affairs, filled with feasting, dancing, and entertainment (Edmondson, 1996). The celebrations would typically last for several days, with various rituals and customs observed throughout. The bride wore a flame-colored veil called the "flammeum" and her hair was styled in six braids to symbolize her virginity (Dixon, 2001). She also donned a special belt, tied in the "knot of Hercules," which her husband would later untie as a symbol of her transition from maidenhood to married life (Kiefer, 2003).

The ceremony itself involved the exchanging of vows, the presentation of a written marriage contract, and the joining of hands (dextrarum iunctio) as a symbol of unity (Treggiari, 1991). A sacrifice to the gods was often made to ensure divine blessings for the newlyweds (Barton, 2001). It was followed by a raucous procession to the couple's new home, with the groom carrying his bride over the threshold to ward off evil spirits (Evans Grubbs, 2002).

Marital Life and Responsibilities

Marital life in Ancient Rome came with a set of duties and responsibilities for both husband and wife. The husband was expected to provide for his family, while the wife was responsible for managing the household and raising their children (Dixon, 2001). Women often played an active role in their husband's business and political affairs, offering advice and support (Rawson, 1986).

The Intriguing World of Roman Adultery

Adultery was not an uncommon occurrence in Ancient Rome. In fact, it was an accepted part of society, as long as certain rules were followed (McGinn, 1998). For instance, adultery was only considered a serious offense if it involved a Roman citizen's wife or daughter, as it could threaten the legitimacy of the family line (Cantarella, 1996).

Emperor Augustus introduced the Lex Iulia de adulteriis (18 BCE), which aimed to control adultery and promote family values (Treggiari, 1991). Under this law, the husband was required to divorce his wife if he discovered her infidelity, and he had the right to kill the adulterer under specific circumstances (McGinn, 1998). Moreover, both the adulterous wife and her lover were subject to exile and the confiscation of their property (Cantarella, 1996).

However, this didn't stop the Romans from engaging in extramarital affairs. In fact, it was not uncommon for Roman men to have relationships with slaves, prostitutes, or even actresses, as these were not considered adulterous (McGinn, 2004). Roman women, on the other hand, had to be more discreet, often engaging in secret affairs with other men or engaging in same-sex relationships to avoid detection (Clarke, 2003).

Adultery and the Roman Elite: Scandal and Hypocrisy
The upper echelons of Roman society were rife with adultery and scandal. It was not uncommon for powerful men to engage

in extramarital affairs, using their status to shield themselves from the consequences (Barton, 2001). The famous statesman Julius Caesar, for example, had numerous affairs with high-profile women, including the wives of his political allies and enemies (Goldsworthy, 2006). His affair with the Egyptian queen Cleopatra was particularly notorious and became a topic of gossip and intrigue throughout Rome (Fletcher, 2008).

Roman emperors were no exception to this rule. Emperor Nero was known for his scandalous love life, which included multiple marriages, affairs, and even accusations of incest (Champlin, 2003). The philandering of these powerful men often served to highlight the hypocrisy of their own laws and the double standards applied to the elite and the common people (Barton, 2001).

The Role of Roman Literature in Depicting Adultery

Roman literature often explored themes of adultery, offering a window into the societal attitudes and expectations of the time. The famous poet Ovid, for example, composed the Amores, a series of love poems that celebrated illicit affairs and the thrill of forbidden love (Ovid, 2002). Similarly, the satirical works of Juvenal and Martial often poked fun at the rampant adultery among the Roman upper classes, highlighting the hypocrisy and moral decay of their society (Juvenal, 1998; Martial, 2003).

Adultery as a Political Weapon: Accusations and Public Image

Accusations of adultery could be used as a political weapon in Ancient Rome, particularly against high-ranking women. Charges of sexual misconduct were often employed to tarnish the reputations of powerful women and weaken their influence (Bauman, 1992). For instance, the Roman historian Tacitus tells the story of Agrippina the Younger, the mother of Emperor Nero, who faced numerous accusations of adultery and incest in an effort to undermine her political power (Tacitus, 2009).

Adultery was an integral part of Roman society, with its own complex rules and expectations. While the Roman elite often engaged in extramarital affairs, they were also held to different standards than the common people, reflecting the moral complexities and contradictions of their society. The exploration of adultery in Roman literature and its use as a political weapon demonstrate the enduring fascination and intrigue surrounding this aspect of Roman life.

Divorce: An Easy Way Out

Divorce was relatively easy to obtain in Ancient Rome, and it was considered a practical solution for unhappy marriages (Gardner, 1986). There was no social stigma attached to divorce, and both men and women could initiate the process. However, the reasons for divorce varied depending on the individual's social status and gender (Treggiari, 1991).

For men, the primary reasons for seeking a divorce were adultery, infertility, or simply falling out of love (Potter, 2009). Meanwhile, women could initiate divorce if their husbands were abusive, adulterous, or if they failed to provide financial support (Gardner, 1991). It is important to note that in both cases, the initiator had to return the dowry to their spouse (Treggiari, 1991).

Interestingly, Roman law even allowed for "trial marriages" known as "usus," where a couple could live together for a year without any legal obligations (Dixon, 2001). If the couple decided to separate within that year, they could do so without any formalities. However, if they lived together for more than a year, they were automatically considered legally married (Shelton, 1988).

Conclusion: A Complex Web of Roman Relationships

The world of Roman relationships was far from simple, but it was also not without passion and intrigue. Marriage, adultery, and divorce were all integral aspects of Roman society, revealing a culture that was both morally flexible and surprisingly progressive in some respects (Potter, 2009). As we've seen in this chapter, the Romans navigated the intricacies of love and desire in their own unique way, giving us a fascinating glimpse into their secret sex lives.

References

Barton, C. A. (2001). Roman Honor: The Fire in the Bones. University of California Press.

Bradley, K. R. (1991). Discovering the Roman Family: Studies in Roman Social History. Oxford University Press.

Cantarella, E. (1996). Pandora's Daughters: The Role and Status of Women in Greek and Roman Antiquity. Johns Hopkins University Press.

Champlin, E. (2003). Nero. Harvard University Press.

Clarke, J. R. (2003). Roman Sex: 100 B.C. to A.D. 250. Harry N. Abrams.

Dixon, S. (2001). Reading Roman Women. Duckworth Publishers.

Edmondson, J. (1996). Roman Home Life and its Influence. In J. Edmondson, & A. Keith (Eds.), Roman Dress and the Fabrics of Roman Culture (pp. 87-106). University of Toronto Press.

Evans Grubbs, J. (2002). Women and the Law in the Roman Empire: A Sourcebook on Marriage, Divorce and Widowhood. Routledge.

Fletcher, J. (2008). Cleopatra the Great: The Woman Behind the Legend. HarperCollins.

Gardner, J. F. (1986). Women in Roman Law and Society. Indiana University Press.
Gardner, J. F. (1991). Divorce in Roman Law. In B. Rawson (Ed.), Marriage, Divorce, and Children in Ancient Rome (pp. 25-48). Oxford University Press.

Goldsworthy, A. (2006). Caesar: Life of a Colossus. Yale University Press.

Kiefer, O. (2003). Sexual Life in Ancient Rome. Routledge.

McGinn, T. A. (1998). Prostitution, Sexuality, and the Law in Ancient Rome. Oxford University Press.

McGinn, T. A. (2004). The Economy of Prostitution in the Roman World: A Study of Social History and the Brothel. University of Michigan Press.

Potter, D. S. (2009). A Companion to the Roman Empire. Wiley-Blackwell.

Rawson, B. (1986). The Family in Ancient Rome: New Perspectives. Cornell University Press.

Shelton, J. (1988). As the Romans Did: A Sourcebook in Roman Social History. Oxford University Press.

Treggiari, S. (1991). Roman Marriage: Iusti Coniuges from the Time of Cicero to the Time of Ulpian. Clarendon Press.

The Brothels of Rome: Prostitution and the Sex Trade

Delve into the hidden corners of ancient Rome as we explore the thriving and often controversial world of Roman brothels, prostitution, and the sex trade. Through captivating narratives and fascinating insights, we'll bring to life the sights, sounds, and scents of the Roman brothels and reveal the complex interplay of power, desire, and commerce that characterized this integral aspect of Roman society. In this exploration, we will examine the lives and experiences of the women and men who worked in the shadows, providing pleasure and companionship to Romans of all social classes.

The Roman Brothel: A Hub of Pleasure and Commerce

Roman brothels, or "lupanaria," were bustling centers of commercial activity and social interaction, frequented by patrons from all walks of life (McGinn, 2004; Veyne, 1987). From soldiers and slaves to politicians and merchants, these establishments catered to the diverse needs and desires of their clientele, offering a wide range of services, from simple conversation and companionship to more erotic and sensual pleasures.

The Architecture and Atmosphere of the Lupanar

The typical Roman brothel was a modest and unassuming building, often located in busy commercial areas or near public baths and theaters (Clarke, 2003; McGinn, 2004). Inside, the lupanar featured a series of small, private rooms or "cubicula," each furnished with a bed and adorned with suggestive frescoes and inscriptions that advertised the specialties and skills of the women who worked there (Clarke, 2003). One such example is the famous Lupanar of Pompeii, where archaeologists discovered numerous erotic frescoes depicting various sexual acts (Wallace-Hadrill, 1994). The atmosphere in the brothel was one of camaraderie and conviviality, with patrons and prostitutes mingling freely, sharing stories, laughter, and intimacy.

The Economics of the Roman Sex Trade

The Roman sex trade was a highly profitable and competitive business, with brothel owners, or "lenones," vying for the patronage of wealthy and influential clients (McGinn, 2004). Prostitutes, or "meretrices," were often slaves or freedwomen who worked to support themselves and their families, earning a steady income through their services and sometimes even achieving a measure of financial independence and social mobility (Veyne, 1987). Prices for their services varied

Satyr and Maenad. Roman fresco from Casa degli Epigrammi in Pompeii. Museo Archeologico Nazionale (Naples)

depending on the prostitute's status, attractiveness, and skills, with high-class courtesans, or "hetaerae," commanding considerable sums from their elite clientele (McGinn, 2004).

The Lives of Roman Prostitutes: Struggles, Triumphs, and Ambiguities

The women who worked in the Roman sex trade faced numerous challenges and hardships, including social stigma, legal restrictions, and the ever-present threat of violence and exploitation (McGinn, 2004). However, they also demonstrated remarkable resilience and resourcefulness, carving out a space for themselves in a society that both desired and disdained their services (Veyne, 1987).

Social Status and the Roman Prostitute
Roman prostitutes occupied a precarious position in society, caught between the allure of their profession and the disdain of a culture that valued chastity and virtue (McGinn, 2004; Veyne, 1987). Despite being viewed as social outcasts, some meretrices managed to transcend the stigma of their occupation and achieve a measure of social respectability. One example is the famed poetess Sulpicia, whose witty and erotic verses earned her a place among Rome's literary elite (Skinner, 2005). However, many other prostitutes remained trapped in a cycle of poverty and marginalization, with few opportunities for advancement or escape.

Love, Friendship, and the Roman Prostitute
Despite the many challenges they faced, Roman prostitutes were not without their moments of joy and companionship.

Many formed close bonds with their fellow workers, sharing laughter, tears, and camaraderie in the face of adversity (McGinn, 2004). Some even found love and romance with their clients, forging deep and enduring connections that transcended the boundaries of social class and moral convention (Veyne, 1987; Fleming, 1999). For instance, the famous Roman general Mark Antony was said to have fallen in love with a high-class prostitute named Cytheris, who later became his mistress and accompanied him on his military campaigns (Plutarch, 1916).

Sexual Practices and Fantasies in the Roman Brothel

The Roman brothel offered a wide range of sexual experiences, catering to the diverse tastes and desires of its clientele. From sensual massage and erotic role-play to more adventurous and exotic practices, the lupanar was a space of exploration and indulgence, where the boundaries of convention and propriety were often pushed to their limits.

Erotic Role-Play and Fantasy Fulfillment

Many Roman brothels catered to their clients' fantasies and desires by offering role-play scenarios and erotic performances (McGinn, 2004). This could involve the prostitute dressing up as a mythological figure or embodying a particular archetype, such as the innocent maiden or the experienced seductress. In some cases, the performance might even take on a theatrical quality, with the client and prostitute acting out a scripted scene or scenario for their mutual pleasure and enjoyment.

Exotic and Adventurous Practices

For those seeking more exotic and adventurous experiences, Roman brothels offered a range of services that pushed the boundaries of conventional sexuality. This could include practices such as group sex, voyeurism, and BDSM, with the meretrices using a variety of tools and techniques to arouse and stimulate their clients (McGinn, 2004; Veyne, 1987). In some cases, these experiences were tinged with an element of danger or transgression, adding to their appeal and allure.

The Role of Brothels in Roman Society

The Roman brothel was more than just a place of vice and debauchery; it played a vital role in the social, cultural, and economic life of the ancient city. From providing a space for social interaction and networking to serving as a focal point for artistic and literary expression, the lupanar was an integral part of the fabric of Roman society.

Brothels as Social Spaces

Roman brothels were not only places where people engaged in sexual activity; they also served as social hubs where patrons could meet, mingle, and forge new connections (McGinn, 2004; Veyne, 1987). This was particularly true for lower-class Romans, who often had limited access to more formal and exclusive social venues, such as the public baths and theaters. In this sense, the lupanar functioned as a kind of "great equalizer," allowing individuals from all strata of society to come together in pursuit of pleasure and camaraderie.

The Brothel in Roman Art and Literature

The world of the Roman brothel was a rich source of inspiration for artists and writers, who drew on its sensual and erotic themes to create works of enduring beauty and power. From the erotic frescoes and inscriptions found in the ruins of Pompeii to the passionate verses of poets such as Ovid, Catullus, and Martial, the brothel loomed large in the Roman imagination, serving as a symbol of both desire and transgression (Wallace-Hadrill, 1994; Ovid, 2008; Catullus, 1990; Martial, 1993). These works often celebrated the sensuality and allure of the Roman prostitute, while also acknowledging the darker aspects of their lives and experiences.

Conclusion: The Brothels of Rome and the Complexities of Desire

As we've seen in this exploration, the brothels of ancient Rome were more than just places of vice and debauchery; they were vibrant and dynamic spaces where people from all walks of life came together in pursuit of pleasure, companionship, and connection.

The stories and experiences of Roman prostitutes reveal the resilience and resourcefulness of individuals who navigated a society that both desired and disdained their services. By examining the lives and struggles of these remarkable women, we gain a deeper understanding of the human experience in ancient Rome, with all its contradictions, challenges, and triumphs.

An erotic scene from a fresco of Pompeii, 50-79 AD.

References

Catullus, G. V. (1990). The Poems of Catullus: A Bilingual Edition. University of California Press.

Clarke, J. R. (2003). Art in the Lives of Ordinary Romans: Visual Representation and Non-elite Viewers in Italy, 100 B.C.–A.D. 315. University of California Press.

Fleming, K. (1999). Love, Romance, and Marriage in Ancient Rome. Archaeology, 52(6), 28–33.

Martial, M. V. (1993). The Epigrams of Martial. Penguin Classics.

McGinn, T. A. (2004). The Economy of Prostitution in the Roman World: A Study of Social History and the Brothel. University of Michigan Press.

Ovid. (2008). The Art of Love: And Other Poems. Loeb Classical Library.

Plutarch. (1916). Plutarch's Lives, Volume 9: Demetrius and Antony. Pyrrhus and Gaius Marius. Loeb Classical Library.

Skinner, M. B. (2005). Sexuality in Greek and Roman Culture. Blackwell Publishing.

Veyne, P. (1987). Roman Erotic Elegy: Love, Poetry, and the West. University of Chicago Press.

Wallace-Hadrill, A. (1994). Houses and Society in Pompeii and Herculaneum. Princeton University Press.

Sexual Symbols: The Roman Way to Love

The Romans were no strangers to love and desire, and they often used symbols, and erotic art to express their passions and enhance their romantic experiences. In this chapter, we will explore the fascinating world of Roman sexual symbols, delving into the customs, beliefs, and practices that shaped their approach to love and lust.

Sexual Symbols: From Priapus to Fascinum

Sexual symbols played a significant role in Roman culture, serving as both decorative elements and objects of worship. The most famous Roman sexual symbol was Priapus, the god of fertility, who was often depicted with an exaggerated, erect phallus (Richlin, 1992). Statues and images of Priapus adorned

Fresco of Priapus, Casa dei Vettii, Pompeii. Depicted weighing his huge penis against a bag of gold.

gardens, homes, and even public spaces, serving as a symbol of protection and abundance (Clarke, 2003).

Another prevalent sexual symbol in Roman culture was the fascinum, a phallic amulet believed to possess magical powers (Johns, 1982). Worn as necklaces or hung in homes, fascinum were thought to protect against the evil eye and bring good fortune (Clarke, 2007). Both men and women, including children, wore these amulets, demonstrating the pervasive nature of sexual symbolism in Roman society (Johns, 1982).

Erotic art was also a common feature of Roman life, adorning everything from frescoes to pottery (Varone, 2001). These explicit images often depicted scenes of lovemaking, as well as humorous or fantastical elements, reflecting the Romans' open-minded attitudes towards sexuality (Clarke, 1998).

Sexual Education and Etiquette

Roman society was relatively open about matters of sex and desire, with sexual education forming an essential aspect of a young person's upbringing (Rawson, 2003). Parents often provided their children with explicit guidance on lovemaking, grooming, and other aspects of sexual behavior, ensuring that they were well-prepared for their future romantic lives (Laes, 2011).

Sexual etiquette, too, was an important part of Roman society, with various rules and customs dictating how couples should behave during intimate encounters (Veyne, 1987). For example, it was considered improper for a man to be too eager or aggressive during lovemaking, while women were expected to maintain an air of modesty and restraint (Veyne, 1987). Mutual consent and pleasure were highly valued, with the understanding that a successful sexual encounter required both partners to be attentive to each other's needs and desires (Richlin, 1992).

The Role of Sexuality in Roman Religion

Sexuality played a significant role in Roman religion, with various deities associated with love, fertility, and desire (Staples, 1998). Venus, the goddess of love, was one of the most revered figures in Roman mythology, and her cult enjoyed immense popularity throughout the empire (Beard, 1996). Worship of Venus often involved the use of aphrodisiacs, sexual symbols, and erotic art, demonstrating the close link between religious devotion and sensual pleasure in Roman society (Staples, 1998).

In addition to Venus, other Roman deities, such as Bacchus (the god of wine and ecstasy) and Cupid (the god of desire), were associated with love and passion (Rosenstein, 1997). Festivals and rituals dedicated to these gods often involved the consumption of aphrodisiacs, as well as the use of sexual symbols and erotic performances (Beard, 1996).

Conclusion: The Roman Way to Love

As we've seen in this chapter, the Romans embraced sexuality with open arms, incorporating it into various aspects of their culture, religion, and daily life. Through the use of sexual symbols, and erotic art, the Romans sought to enhance their romantic experiences and express their desires in creative and imaginative ways. This fascinating blend of sensuality and spirituality offers a unique insight into the Roman way to love, revealing a society that celebrated passion and desire in all its forms.

References

Beard, M. (1996). Rome in the Late Republic. Cornell University Press.

Betz, H. D. (1996). The Greek Magical Papyri in Translation, Including the Demotic Spells. University of Chicago Press.

Clarke, J. R. (1998). Looking at Lovemaking: Constructions of Sexuality in Roman Art, 100 B.C. to A.D. 250. University of California Press.

Clarke, J. R. (2003). Roman Sex: 100 B.C. to A.D. 250. Harry N. Abrams.

Clarke, J. R. (2007). Roman Life: 100 B.C. to A.D. 250. Harry N. Abrams.

Dalby, A. (2003). Food in the Ancient World from A to Z. Routledge.

Flower, M. A. (2008). The Seer in Ancient Greece. University of California Press.

Grainger, S. (2005). Cooking Apicius: Roman Recipes for Today. Serif.

Johns, C. (1982). Sex or Symbol: Erotic Images of Greece and Rome. British Museum Publications.

Laes, C. (2011). Children in the Roman Empire: Outsiders Within. Cambridge University Press.

Rawson, B. (2003). Children and Childhood in Roman Italy. Oxford University Press.

Richlin, A. (1992). The Garden of Priapus: Sexuality and Aggression in Roman Humor. Oxford University Press.

Rosenstein, N. S. (1997). Imperatores Victi: Military Defeat and Aristocratic Competition in the Middle and Late Republic. University of California Press.

Staples, A. (1998). From Good Goddess to Vestal Virgins: Sex and Category in Roman Religion. Routledge.

Varone, A. (2001). Erotica Pompeiana: Love Inscriptions on the Walls of Pompeii. L'Erma di Bretschneider.

Veyne, P. (1987). Roman Erotic Elegy: Love, Poetry, and the West. University of Chicago Press.

Gods, Goddesses, and Fertility Cults: Religion and Sexuality

Religion and sexuality were deeply intertwined in Ancient Rome, with numerous gods, goddesses, and fertility cults playing a central role in shaping the culture's approach to love and desire. In this chapter, we will delve into the fascinating world of Roman religious beliefs and practices related to sexuality, exploring the intricate web of myth, ritual, and symbolism that formed the foundation of Roman attitudes towards sex and sensuality.

Venus: The Goddess of Love and Beauty

Venus, the Roman goddess of love and beauty, was one of the most revered deities in the pantheon, with her cult enjoying immense popularity throughout the empire (Beard, 1996). As the embodiment of love, passion, and desire, Venus played a

Fresco from Pompei, Casa di Venus, CE.1st century.

central role in Roman sexuality, influencing everything from marriage rituals to aphrodisiac recipes (Staples, 1998).

The Romans believed that Venus had the power to inspire love and desire in both mortals and gods alike, with numerous myths recounting her amorous adventures and romantic entanglements (Ovid, 2003). One of the most famous tales is the story of Venus and Mars, the god of war, who engaged in a passionate affair that resulted in the birth of Cupid, the god of desire (Hesiod, 2006).

Venus was also closely associated with fertility and reproduction, and many Roman women sought her aid in matters of childbirth and conception (Staples, 1998). In this capacity, Venus was often depicted holding a baby or accompanied by her son, Cupid, symbolizing her role as the divine mother of love and procreation (Beard, 1996).

Worship of Venus often involved the use of sexual symbols, aphrodisiacs, and erotic art, demonstrating the close link between religious devotion and sensual pleasure in Roman society (Staples, 1998). For example, devotees of Venus would often wear amulets depicting the goddess in erotic poses, believing that these images would attract love and passion into their lives (Clarke, 2007).

Bacchus: The God of Wine and Ecstasy

Bacchus, the Roman god of wine and ecstasy, was another influential figure in the realm of Roman sexuality (Rosenstein, 1997). As the patron deity of intoxication, Bacchus was believed to possess the power to unleash the primal forces of desire and sensuality, liberating his followers from the constraints of reason and morality (Otto, 1965).

The cult of Bacchus was famed for its wild, uninhibited celebrations, known as Bacchanalia, which often involved the consumption of large quantities of wine, ecstatic dancing, and sexual revelry (Rosenstein, 1997). These orgiastic rites were believed to facilitate communion with the divine, allowing the participants to experience the ecstatic union of body and spirit (Otto, 1965).

In addition to his role as the god of wine and ecstasy, Bacchus was also associated with fertility and agriculture, and his cult often incorporated phallic symbols and fertility rituals into its practices (Beard, 1996). For example, during the annual festival of Liberalia, the followers of Bacchus would carry a large phallus through the streets, symbolizing the regenerative powers of the god and his connection to the natural world (Rosenstein, 1997).

Cupid: The God of Desire

Cupid, the Roman god of desire, played a crucial role in the culture's approach to love and passion, embodying the irresistible force of attraction that binds lovers together (Ovid, 2003). Often depicted as a mischievous, winged youth armed with a bow and arrow, Cupid was believed to possess the power to inspire love and desire in both mortals and gods, with his arrows causing uncontrollable passion in those they struck (Hesiod, 2006).

Cupid's amorous exploits were a popular theme in Roman art and literature, with numerous tales recounting his adventures and romantic escapades (Ovid, 2003). One of the most famous stories is that of Cupid and Psyche, a mortal woman who falls in love with the god after being struck by one of his arrows (Apuleius, 2008), which we looked at in more detail earlier in the book.

Fertility Cults: From the Lupercalia to the Floralia

Fertility cults played a significant role in Roman religion, with numerous festivals and rituals dedicated to the celebration of procreation, growth, and abundance (Beard, 1996). These cults often incorporated sexual symbols, aphrodisiacs, and erotic performances into their practices, demonstrating the close link between religious devotion and sensual pleasure in Roman society (Staples, 1998).

One of the most famous fertility festivals in Ancient Rome was the Lupercalia, an annual celebration held in February to honor the god Lupercus and ensure the fertility of the land and its people (Wiseman, 1995). During the festival, young men dressed in the skins of sacrificed animals would run through the streets, whipping women with strips of hide to ensure their fertility and promote a healthy pregnancy (Wiseman, 1995).

Another popular fertility festival was the Floralia, a celebration held in April to honor Flora, the goddess of flowers and springtime (Beard, 1996). This festival featured processions, theatrical performances, and the release of hares and goats, which were symbols of fertility (Beard, 1996). The Floralia was also renowned for its erotic elements, with prostitutes and courtesans playing a prominent role in the festivities, performing lascivious dances and engaging in various acts of exhibitionism (Clarke, 2007).

Conclusion: Religion and Sexuality in Ancient Rome

As we have seen in this chapter, the worlds of religion and sexuality were deeply interconnected in Ancient Rome, with gods, goddesses, and fertility cults playing a central role in shaping the culture's approach to love and desire. Through the worship of deities like Venus, Bacchus, and Cupid, and the celebration of fertility festivals such as the Lupercalia and the Floralia, the Romans sought to honor the divine powers of love, passion, and procreation that governed their lives.

This intricate web of myth, ritual, and symbolism reveals a culture that viewed sexuality as both a sacred gift and a divine mystery, an expression of the eternal dance between the human and the divine. By exploring the rich tapestry of Roman religious beliefs and practices related to sexuality, we gain a deeper understanding of the culture's unique approach to love and desire, offering a fascinating glimpse into the sacred realm of Roman passion and sensuality.

References

Apuleius. (2008). The Golden Ass. Oxford University Press.

Beard, M. (1996). Rome in the Late Republic. Cornell University Press.

Clarke, J. R. (2007). Roman Life: 100 B.C. to A.D. 250. Harry N. Abrams.

Gaisser, J. H. (1998). The Fortunes of Apuleius and the Golden Ass: A Study in Transmission and Reception. Princeton University Press.

Hesiod. (2006). Theogony and Works and Days. Oxford University Press.

Ovid. (2003). The Erotic Poems. Penguin Classics.

Otto, W. F. (1965). Dionysus: Myth and Cult. Indiana University Press.

Rosenstein, N. S. (1997). Imperatores Victi: Military Defeat and Aristocratic Competition in the Middle and Late Republic. University of California Press.
Staples, A. (1998). From Good Goddess to Vestal Virgins: Sex and Category in Roman Religion. Routledge.

Wiseman, T. P. (1995). Remus: A Roman Myth. Cambridge University Press.

Homosexuality in Ancient Rome: Love, Desire, and Acceptance

Homosexuality in Ancient Rome presents a complex and fascinating picture of love, desire, and acceptance. Despite the rigid social hierarchies and moral codes that governed Roman society, same-sex relationships and erotic encounters were a prominent feature of the culture, permeating various aspects of daily life, art, and literature. In this chapter, we will explore the multifaceted world of homosexuality in Ancient Rome, examining the diverse range of attitudes, beliefs, and practices that shaped the culture's approach to love and desire between individuals of the same sex.

Homosexuality in Roman Literature and Art

Homosexuality was a prevalent theme in Roman literature and art, with numerous authors, poets, and artists exploring the complexities of same-sex love and desire in their works (Clarke, 1998). From the erotic elegies of Catullus and Tibullus to the satirical writings of Juvenal and Martial, the Roman literary tradition abounds with tales of amorous encounters, romantic trysts, and passionate affairs between men (Richlin, 1992).

One of the most famous examples of homosexuality in Roman literature is the relationship between the poet Virgil and his beloved Alexis, a young male slave who served as the inspiration for many of Virgil's most passionate and poignant verses (Virgil, 2001). The love between Virgil and Alexis, which is celebrated in numerous poems and elegies, offers a striking testament to the depth and intensity of same-sex desire in Ancient Rome (Williams, 2010).

Roman art also provides a rich and vivid portrayal of homosexuality, with numerous frescoes, mosaics, and sculptures depicting scenes of same-sex love and eroticism (Clarke, 1998). One of the most famous examples of homosexual imagery in Roman art is the www, a silver drinking vessel that features two explicit scenes of male-male lovemaking (Vout, 2007). This remarkable artifact, which dates back to the 1st century AD, offers a tantalizing glimpse into the sensual world of Roman homosexuality, revealing a culture that celebrated the beauty and passion of same-sex desire.

HOMOSEXUALITY IN ANCIENT ROME: LOVE, DESIRE, AND ACCEPTANCE

Two sides of the Warren Cup depicting homosexual intercourse; mid 1st century AD.

Roman Attitudes Towards Homosexuality: A Complex Picture

While homosexuality was a prominent feature of Roman culture, attitudes towards same-sex relationships and erotic encounters were complex and multifaceted, shaped by a diverse array of social, political, and moral factors (Williams, 2010). On the one hand, homosexuality was widely accepted and tolerated, with same-sex love and desire viewed as a natural and integral part of human experience (Cantarella, 2002). On the other hand, Roman society was governed by a strict code of sexual ethics and social hierarchies, which placed certain restrictions on the expression of same-sex desire and the formation of homosexual relationships (Richlin, 1992).

One of the key factors that influenced Roman attitudes towards homosexuality was the culture's emphasis on the ideals of masculinity and male virtue, which prized qualities such as strength, courage, and self-control (Williams, 2010). In this context, homosexuality was often viewed as a threat to the traditional values of Roman society, with same-sex relationships seen as a potential source of moral corruption and social disorder (Cantarella, 2002).

However, this negative view of homosexuality was not universal, and many Romans embraced same-sex desire as a natural and essential aspect of human sexuality (Cantarella, 2002). In fact, some of the most famous and revered figures in Roman history, such as Julius Caesar, Hadrian, and the poet Horace, were known to have engaged in homosexual relationships or expressed same-sex desire in their works (Williams, 2010).

Another important factor that shaped Roman attitudes towards homosexuality was the culture's distinction between the roles of the 'active' and 'passive' partners in a same-sex relationship (Richlin, 1992). According to Roman sexual norms, the 'active' partner, typically an older, more dominant male, was seen as the embodiment of masculine virtues, while the 'passive' partner, usually a younger, more submissive male or a slave, was considered the object of desire and sexual gratification (Williams, 2010). This hierarchical approach to homosexuality allowed the Romans to reconcile their acceptance of same-sex desire with their commitment to traditional gender roles and social norms (Cantarella, 2002).

Homosexuality and the Roman Elite: Love, Desire, and Scandal

The Roman elite played a crucial role in shaping the culture's approach to homosexuality, with their amorous exploits, romantic liaisons, and erotic adventures providing a fascinating insight into the world of same-sex desire in Ancient Rome (Clarke, 1998). While homosexuality was not universally accepted among the upper classes, many members of the aristocracy engaged in same-sex relationships or indulged in homosexual encounters, often as a means of asserting their social status and asserting their power over their subordinates (Williams, 2010).

One of the most famous examples of homosexuality among the Roman elite is the relationship between the Emperor Hadrian and his beloved Antinous, a young Greek youth who became the object of the emperor's passionate devotion (Vout, 2007).

The love between Hadrian and Antinous, which is celebrated in numerous statues, coins, and inscriptions, offers a striking example of the acceptance and celebration of same-sex desire among the Roman aristocracy (Vout, 2007).

However, not all homosexual relationships among the Roman elite were met with such tolerance and admiration, and many same-sex liaisons were the subject of scandal and controversy (Clarke, 1998). For example, the affair between the famous orator Cicero and his protege, Marcus Caelius Rufus, was widely condemned by their contemporaries, who accused Cicero of corrupting the young man and using him for his own sexual gratification (Wiseman, 1987).

Homosexuality and Roman Law: Tolerance and Persecution

Roman law offers a complex and often contradictory picture of the culture's approach to homosexuality, with legal statutes and court rulings reflecting the diverse range of attitudes, beliefs, and practices that shaped the Romans' understanding of same-sex desire (Cantarella, 2002). On the one hand, Roman law was relatively tolerant of homosexuality, with no specific provisions criminalizing same-sex relationships or erotic encounters (Richlin, 1992). On the other hand, the Roman legal system imposed certain restrictions on the expression of homosexuality, with laws governing marriage, adoption, and citizenship placing limits on the rights and freedoms of individuals engaged in same-sex relationships (Williams, 2010).

One of the key areas in which Roman law addressed homosexuality was the regulation of marriage and family life, which was governed by a strict code of sexual ethics and moral values (Cantarella, 2002). According to Roman marriage law, same-sex couples were not permitted to marry, and individuals engaged in homosexual relationships were often denied the same legal rights and protections afforded to their heterosexual counterparts (Williams, 2010).

Despite these legal restrictions, Roman society was largely tolerant of homosexuality, with same-sex relationships and erotic encounters rarely subject to legal persecution or punishment (Cantarella, 2002). However, there were exceptions to this general rule of tolerance, particularly during periods of political turmoil or moral panic, when homosexuality was sometimes targeted as a scapegoat for social ills and perceived moral decline (Richlin, 1992).

For example, during the reign of Emperor Domitian, a number of prominent individuals were accused of engaging in homosexual acts and subsequently executed or exiled as a result of their alleged transgressions (Jones, 1992). Similarly, the Emperor Theodosius I enacted legislation that criminalized certain forms of homosexual behavior, particularly those involving the seduction or corruption of freeborn youths (Cantarella, 2002).

Conclusion: Love, Desire, and Acceptance in Ancient Rome

As we have seen in this chapter, homosexuality in Ancient

Rome presents a rich and diverse tapestry of love, desire, and acceptance, offering a fascinating insight into the culture's unique approach to same-sex relationships and erotic encounters. From the passionate verses of Virgil and the sensual imagery of Roman art to the complex legal and social norms that governed same-sex desire, the world of Roman homosexuality reveals a culture that both celebrated and challenged the boundaries of love, passion, and desire.

This intricate web of attitudes, beliefs, and practices sheds light on the complexities of Roman society, revealing a culture that was at once deeply conservative and remarkably open-minded in its approach to sexuality and human relationships. By exploring the multifaceted world of homosexuality in Ancient Rome, we gain a deeper understanding of the culture's distinctive approach to love, desire, and acceptanc.

References

Cantarella, E. (2002). Bisexuality in the Ancient World. Yale University Press.

Clarke, J. R. (1998). Looking at Lovemaking: Constructions of Sexuality in Roman Art, 100 B.C. - A.D. 250. University of California Press.

Jones, B. W. (1992). The Emperor Domitian. Routledge.

Richlin, A. (1992). The Garden of Priapus: Sexuality and Aggression in Roman Humor. Oxford University Press.

Virgil. (2001). The Eclogues. Penguin Classics.

Vout, C. (2007). Power and Eroticism in Imperial Rome. Cambridge University Press.

Williams, C. A. (2010). Roman Homosexuality: Ideologies of Masculinity in Classical Antiquity. Oxford University Press.

Wiseman, T. P. (1987). Clio's Cosmetics: Three Studies in Greco-Roman Literature. Leicester University Press.

Pederasty and the Roman Elite: Power Dynamics and Mentorship

Pederasty, the practice of romantic and sexual relationships between adult men and adolescent boys, has been a prominent feature of many ancient cultures, including Greece, Rome, and Persia. In Ancient Rome, pederasty played a significant role in the lives of the elite, serving as both a means of asserting power and dominance and a form of mentorship and guidance for young men entering adulthood. In this chapter, we will explore the complex world of pederasty among the Roman elite, examining the power dynamics, social norms, and cultural practices that shaped this unique form of same-sex desire and mentorship.

Pederasty in Roman Literature and Art

Roman literature and art offer a wealth of evidence for the practice of pederasty among the elite, with numerous authors, poets, and artists exploring the complexities of these relationships in their works (Cantarella, 2002). From the passionate elegies of Catullus and the satirical verses of Martial to the historical writings of Suetonius and Tacitus, the Roman literary tradition abounds with references to pederastic relationships, revealing the diverse range of attitudes and beliefs that shaped the culture's understanding of this practice (Williams, 2010).

One of the most famous examples of pederasty in Roman literature is the relationship between the poet Horace and his beloved Ligurinus, a young male slave who served as the inspiration for many of Horace's most tender and poignant verses (Horace, 2008). The love between Horace and Ligurinus, which is celebrated in numerous poems and elegies, offers a striking testament to the depth and intensity of pederastic desire in Ancient Rome (Williams, 2010).

Roman art also provides a rich and vivid portrayal of pederasty, with numerous frescoes, mosaics, and sculptures depicting scenes of same-sex love and eroticism between adult men and adolescent boys (Clarke, 1998). Pompeii, for instance, contains a variety of erotic frescoes and artwork that feature scenes with satyrs, some of which engage in sensual encounters with young males. These artifacts, dating back to the 1st century AD, offer glimpses into the sensual world of Roman pederasty, revealing a culture that celebrated the beauty and passion of same-sex desire between men and youths.

Pederasty and the Roman Elite: Power, Dominance, and Mentorship

The Roman elite played a crucial role in shaping the culture's approach to pederasty, with their amorous exploits, romantic liaisons, and erotic adventures providing a fascinating insight into the world of same-sex desire and mentorship in Ancient Rome (Clarke, 1998). While pederasty was not universally accepted among the upper classes, many members of the aristocracy engaged in these relationships or indulged in pederastic encounters, often as a means of asserting their social status and demonstrating their power over their subordinates (Williams, 2010).

One of the key aspects of pederasty among the Roman elite was the power dynamic between the adult male, or 'erastes,' and the adolescent boy, or 'eromenos' (Cantarella, 2002). According to Roman social norms, the erastes was expected to be a dominant and authoritative figure, guiding the eromenos through the challenges and complexities of adolescence and preparing him for the responsibilities and duties of adult life (Williams, 2010). In this context, pederasty served as a form of mentorship, with the erastes acting as a teacher, role model, and protector for the eromenos, imparting essential knowledge, wisdom, and experience to the young man (Cantarella, 2002).

However, the relationship between the erastes and the eromenos was not solely focused on mentorship and guidance; it also involved a strong erotic component, with the adult male expressing his desire and affection for the adolescent boy through acts of physical intimacy and sexual gratification

(Clarke, 1998). In this sense, pederasty among the Roman elite was both a form of power and dominance and a means of nurturing and cultivating the emotional, intellectual, and sexual development of the eromenos (Williams, 2010).

Pederasty and Roman Law: Tolerance and Persecution

Roman law offers a complex and often contradictory picture of the culture's approach to pederasty, with legal statutes and court rulings reflecting the diverse range of attitudes, beliefs, and practices that shaped the Romans' understanding of this practice (Cantarella, 2002). On the one hand, Roman law was relatively tolerant of pederasty, with no specific provisions criminalizing relationships between adult men and adolescent boys (Richlin, 1992). On the other hand, the Roman legal system imposed certain restrictions on the expression of pederastic desire, with laws governing marriage, adoption, and citizenship placing limits on the rights and freedoms of individuals engaged in these relationships (Williams, 2010).

According to Roman marriage law, pederastic relationships were not considered a legitimate form of marital union, and individuals engaged in these relationships were often denied the same legal rights and protections afforded to their heterosexual counterparts (Williams, 2010).

Despite these legal restrictions, Roman society was largely tolerant of pederasty, with relationships between adult men and adolescent boys rarely subject to legal persecution or punishment (Cantarella, 2002). However, there were exceptions to this general rule of tolerance, particularly during periods of political turmoil or moral panic, when pederasty was sometimes targeted as a scapegoat for social ills and perceived moral decline (Richlin, 1992).

For example, during the reign of Emperor Tiberius, a number of prominent individuals were accused of engaging in pederastic acts and subsequently executed or exiled as a result of their alleged transgressions (Tacitus, 2004). Similarly, the Emperor Domitian enacted legislation that criminalized certain forms of pederastic behavior, particularly those involving the seduction or corruption of freeborn youths (Jones, 1992).

Conclusion: Pederasty and the Roman Elite

As we have seen in this chapter, pederasty among the Roman elite presents a complex and multifaceted picture of power dynamics, mentorship, and same-sex desire, offering a fascinating insight into the culture's unique approach to these relationships. From the passionate verses of Horace and the sensual imagery of Roman art to the complex legal and social norms that governed pederastic desire, the world of Roman pederasty reveals a culture that both celebrated and challenged the boundaries of love, passion, and mentorship.

References

Cantarella, E. (2002). Bisexuality in the Ancient World. Yale University Press.

Clarke, J. R. (1998). Looking at Lovemaking: Constructions of Sexuality in Roman Art, 100 B.C. - A.D. 250. University of California Press.

Horace. (2008). The Complete Odes and Epodes. Oxford University Press.

Jones, B. W. (1992). The Emperor Domitian. Routledge.

Richlin, A. (1992). The Garden of Priapus: Sexuality and Aggression in Roman Humor. Oxford University Press.
Tacitus. (2004). The Annals of Imperial Rome. Penguin Classics.

Williams, C. A. (2010). Roman Homosexuality: Ideologies of Masculinity in Classical Antiquity. Oxford University Press.

Roman Sex Education: From Childhood to Adulthood

Sex education in Ancient Rome was a far cry from the structured and formalized programs we are accustomed to in modern times. Instead, Roman sex education took place through a diverse range of informal sources, including family, friends, peers, and even the omnipresent erotic art that adorned the walls of Roman cities (Clarke, 1998). In this chapter, we will embark on a fascinating journey through Roman sex education, exploring how young Romans learned about the mysteries and intricacies of love, desire, and passion from childhood to adulthood.

The Roman Family: A Crucible of Sexual Knowledge

For many young Romans, their first exposure to the world of sex and sexuality came from within the family unit, where parents, siblings, and other relatives provided a rich and varied source of information about the birds and the bees (Rawson, 2003). In the Roman household, sex was often a visible and open aspect of daily life, with family members routinely sharing living spaces, sleeping quarters, and bathing facilities, affording children ample opportunity to observe the intimate and sexual behaviors of their elders (Rawson, 2003).

As Roman children grew older, they would receive more explicit guidance from their parents, who were often responsible for providing the bulk of their sex education (Rawson, 2003). Roman fathers, for example, might instruct their sons on matters of masculine virility and sexual performance, while mothers would typically share their knowledge of feminine sexuality, fertility, and childbirth with their daughters (Cantarella, 2002).

The Role of Peers and Friends in Roman Sex Education

In addition to the family, young Romans would also learn about sex and sexuality from their peers and friends, who played a crucial role in shaping their attitudes, beliefs, and practices in this domain (Rawson, 2003). Through gossip, jokes, and storytelling, young people would share their sexual experiences, fantasies, and desires with one another, forging a collective understanding of the mysteries and complexities of love and desire (Richlin, 1992).

These informal networks of sexual knowledge extended beyond the confines of the family and friendship groups, with young Romans often turning to more experienced members of their community for advice and guidance on matters of the heart (Rawson, 2003). For example, young men might seek the counsel of an older, more experienced male relative or mentor, who could offer valuable insights into the art of seduction, courtship, and lovemaking (Williams, 2010).

Erotic Art and Literature: Windows into Roman Sexuality

One of the most striking aspects of Roman sex education was the prevalence of erotic art and literature, which provided young people with a vivid and often explicit window into the world of Roman sexuality (Clarke, 1998). From the sensual frescoes that adorned the walls of Pompeii to the bawdy verses of Catullus and Martial, the Romans were surrounded by a rich and varied tapestry of erotic imagery and expression, which would have played a significant role in shaping their understanding of sex and desire (Clarke, 1998).

Roman erotic art was characterized by a remarkable degree of realism and detail, with artists capturing a wide range of sexual acts, positions, and scenarios in their works (Clarke, 1998). This artistic tradition, which dates back to the early days of the Republic, offered young Romans a comprehensive and often explicit visual guide to the mechanics and pleasures of sex, providing an invaluable resource for their burgeoning sexual knowledge and curiosity (Clarke, 1998).

Similarly, Roman literature abounded with erotic themes and motifs, with poets, playwrights, and novelists exploring the complexities and nuances of desire, passion, and seduction in their works (Richlin, 1992). From the passionate elegies of Ovid's "Amores" to the bawdy humor of Petronius' "Satyricon," Roman literature offered young people a wealth of insights into the human experience of love and desire, serving as both a source of entertainment and a form of sex education (Richlin, 1992).

Sex Education through Religious Rites and Festivals

Religion played a significant role in Roman sex education, with various rites, ceremonies, and festivals dedicated to gods and goddesses of love, fertility, and sexuality offering young people valuable insights into the sacred dimensions of human desire (Beard, North, & Price, 1998). One of the most famous examples of this is the Lupercalia, an annual festival celebrated in honor of the god Lupercus, who was associated with fertility and purification (Beard et al., 1998). During the Lupercalia, young men would participate in a series of rituals and ceremonies designed to promote fertility and ward off evil spirits, offering them a unique opportunity to engage with the spiritual aspects of sex and reproduction (Beard et al., 1998).

Another example is the cult of Venus, the Roman goddess of love and beauty, whose temples and shrines were scattered throughout the empire and served as a focal point for the worship of love, passion, and desire (Beard et al., 1998). For young Romans seeking to understand the mysteries of the heart, the cult of Venus provided a wealth of knowledge and inspiration, as well as a powerful reminder of the divine nature of human love and attraction (Beard et al., 1998).

Conclusion: Roman Sex Education from Childhood to Adulthood

As we have seen in this chapter, Roman sex education was a multifaceted and diverse phenomenon, encompassing a wide range of sources, influences, and practices. From the intimate guidance of parents and mentors to the vivid imagery of erotic art and the sacred wisdom of religious rites, young Romans were exposed to a rich and varied tapestry of sexual knowledge and experience, which would have shaped their understanding of love, desire, and passion from childhood to adulthood.

Interestingly, there are similarities between Roman sex education and modern sex education, as both rely on various sources, including parents, mentors, friends, and peers, as well as various media and cultural influences, to shape an individual's understanding of sexuality.

Despite the differences in time and culture, it is intriguing to see how the fundamental human need for sexual knowledge and understanding transcends historical boundaries, reminding us of the enduring power and universality of human desire and connection.

References

Beard, M., North, J., & Price, S. (1998). Religions of Rome: Volume 1, A History. Cambridge University Press.

Cantarella, E. (2002). Bisexuality in the Ancient World. Yale University Press.

Clarke, J. R. (1998). Looking at Lovemaking: Constructions of Sexuality in Roman Art, 100 B.C. - A.D. 250. University of California Press.

Rawson, B. (2003). Children and Childhood in Roman Italy. Oxford University Press.

Richlin, A. (1992). The Garden of Priapus: Sexuality and Aggression in Roman Humor. Oxford University Press.

Williams, C. A. (2010). Roman Homosexuality: Ideologies of Masculinity in Classical Antiquity. Oxford University Press.

Gender Roles and Stereotypes: Expectations in Roman Society

The ancient Romans, like many other cultures throughout history, held a set of expectations and assumptions about the roles and behaviors of men and women. Gender roles and stereotypes were deeply ingrained in Roman society, shaping the lives of individuals from birth to death. In this chapter, we will explore the complex world of gender expectations in ancient Rome, delving into the various ways these roles and stereotypes were reinforced and challenged over time.

Roman Masculinity: Virtus, Virility, and the Roman Man

In ancient Rome, masculinity was defined by a set of values, qualities, and expectations that were central to the male experience. At the core of Roman masculinity was the concept of virtus, a Latin term that encompassed ideals such as courage, honor, and strength (Williams, 2010). To be considered a true Roman man, one needed to embody these virtues, both in the public sphere and within the private confines of the family.

In addition to virtus, Roman masculinity was closely associated with virility, or the ability to father children and fulfill one's role as a husband and provider (Gardner, 1991). For Roman men, sexual prowess and fertility were essential aspects of their identity, with the ability to satisfy one's wife and produce offspring serving as key markers of manhood (Gardner, 1991).

Roman men were also expected to assume leadership roles within their households and communities. The paterfamilias, or male head of the family, held considerable authority and responsibility, making decisions about matters such as marriage, property, and inheritance on behalf of his family members (Rawson, 2003). In the political sphere, Roman men were expected to participate in civic life and serve in the military, further reinforcing their roles as leaders and protectors (Williams, 2010).

Roman Femininity: Women, Marriage, and Motherhood

For Roman women, the expectations and stereotypes associated with their gender were focused primarily on their roles as wives, mothers, and caretakers. Roman women were expected to marry and bear children, with their primary duties centered on the home and family (Rawson, 2003). In fact, the Latin word for wife, "mater," is etymologically linked to the word for mother, "materfamilias," underscoring the centrality of motherhood in Roman women's lives (Gardner, 1991).

In addition to their roles as wives and mothers, Roman women were also responsible for managing the household and overseeing the education and upbringing of their children (Rawson, 2003). While Roman men held ultimate authority within the family, women were often the primary caregivers and nurturers, ensuring the well-being and stability of the family unit (Rawson, 2003).

Despite these traditional expectations, Roman women were not entirely confined to the private sphere. In fact, many women in ancient Rome were active participants in public life, engaging in various forms of religious, social, and economic activity (Gardner, 1991). Roman women could own property, run businesses, and even serve as priestesses in religious cults, challenging the notion that their roles were limited exclusively to the home and family (Gardner, 1991).

The Intersection of Class and Gender in Roman Society

The expectations and stereotypes surrounding gender roles in ancient Rome were not uniform across all social strata. Instead, they were influenced by factors such as social class, wealth, and status, which could significantly impact an individual's experience of gender in Roman society (Gardner, 1991).

For example, elite Roman women often enjoyed greater freedom and autonomy than their lower-class counterparts, thanks in part to their elevated social standing and access to resources (Rawson, 2003). While they were still expected to fulfill their roles as wives and mothers, elite Roman women were more likely to have access to education, participate in civic and cultural life, and exert influence over their family's affairs (Gardner, 1991).

Conversely, lower-class Roman women typically faced more restrictive gender expectations and were more limited in their ability to engage in public life or challenge traditional gender roles (Rawson, 2003). Their primary duties were centered on the home and family, with limited opportunities for education, civic engagement, or economic independence (Gardner, 1991).

For Roman men, social class also played a significant role in shaping their experience of masculinity and gender expectations. Elite Roman men were expected to embody the ideal of the virile, authoritative paterfamilias and to participate in political and military life, while lower-class men often faced more limited opportunities for advancement and social mobility (Williams, 2010).

Challenging Gender Stereotypes in Ancient Rome

While gender roles and stereotypes were deeply ingrained in Roman society, there were instances where individuals pushed back against these expectations, challenging the traditional norms and boundaries of their gender. For example, Roman women such as Livia, the wife of Emperor Augustus, and Agrippina the Younger, the mother of Emperor Nero, wielded considerable power and influence in the political sphere, defying the conventional expectations of their gender (Barrett, 2002).

Similarly, some Roman men sought to redefine the parameters of masculinity by engaging in activities or adopting personas that were considered atypical for their gender. For instance, Emperor Hadrian was known for his passion for art and culture, as well as his close relationship with the young male lover Antinous, both of which challenged traditional notions of Roman masculinity (Birley, 1997).

Gender Roles and Stereotypes in Roman Literature and Art

Roman literature and art provide valuable insights into the gender roles and stereotypes that prevailed in ancient Roman society, as well as the ways in which these expectations were reinforced, challenged, and subverted by the Romans themselves.

In literature, works such as Ovid's "Metamorphoses" and "Amores" and the poems of Catullus and Martia, which we looked at earlier in the book, frequently explored themes of love, desire, and gender, offering both conventional and subversive perspectives on Roman masculinity and femininity (Richlin, 1992). Similarly, the plays of Plautus and Terence often portrayed women as clever, resourceful, and independent, challenging traditional gender stereotypes and expectations (McCarthy, 2000).

In the realm of visual art, Roman frescoes, sculptures, and mosaics depicted a wide range of gendered imagery, from heroic male warriors and idealized female beauties to scenes of domestic life and erotic encounters (Clarke, 1998). These artistic representations served to both reinforce and contest the prevailing gender roles and stereotypes in Roman society, offering a complex and multifaceted portrait of Roman gender expectations (Clarke, 1998).

Conclusion: Gender Roles and Stereotypes in Roman Society

As we have seen throughout this chapter, gender roles and stereotypes were a powerful and pervasive force in Roman society, shaping the lives of individuals across a diverse range of social and cultural contexts. From the expectations surrounding masculinity and femininity to the ways in which these roles were reinforced and contested in various aspects of Roman life, gender played a central role in shaping the experiences and identities of the men and women who inhabited this ancient world.

By examining the complex web of gender roles and stereotypes in ancient Rome, we gain a deeper understanding of the social, cultural, and ideological forces that underpinned Roman society, shedding light on the diverse and often surprising ways in which gender expectations were negotiated and navigated by the Romans themselves.

When comparing Roman gender roles and stereotypes to those of the modern era, we can see that there are both similarities and differences. For instance, both Roman and modern societies place value on traditional roles of men as protectors and providers, while women are often expected to fulfill nurturing and caregiving roles. However, in modern times, we have also witnessed a shift towards more equitable gender expectations, with increasing numbers of women taking on leadership roles and men embracing caregiving responsibilities.

Despite these advancements, it is crucial to recognize the persistent influence of gender stereotypes in both Roman and modern societies. This comparison serves as a reminder that the negotiation and navigation of gender roles and expectations is an ongoing process, and one that continues to shape the lives of individuals across different cultures and historical periods.

References

Barrett, A. (2002). Livia: First Lady of Imperial Rome. Yale University Press.

Birley, A. (1997). Hadrian: The Restless Emperor. Routledge.

Clarke, J. R. (1998). Looking at Lovemaking: Constructions of Sexuality in Roman Art, 100 B.C. – A.D. 250. University of California Press.

Gardner, J. F. (1991). Women in Roman Law and Society. Indiana University Press.

McCarthy, K. (2000). Slaves, Masters, and the Art of Authority in Plautine Comedy. Princeton University Press.

Rawson, B. (2003). Children and Childhood in Roman Italy. Oxford University Press.

Richlin, A. (1992). The Garden of Priapus: Sexuality and Aggression in Roman Humor. Oxford University Press.

Williams, C. A. (2010). Roman Homosexuality: Ideologies of Masculinity in Classical Antiquity. Oxford University Press.

Sexual Taboos and Deviance: Crossing the Line

Every society has its limits when it comes to sexuality, and ancient Rome was no exception. While the Romans were known for their open-minded attitudes towards sex, there were still certain practices and behaviors that were considered taboo or deviant. In this chapter, we will explore the fascinating world of sexual taboos and deviance in Roman society, highlighting the ways in which the Romans drew the line between what was considered acceptable and what was deemed to be beyond the pale.

The Dark Side of Roman Eroticism: Prohibitions and Punishments

While Roman society was relatively permissive when it came to sexual expression, there were specific acts and relationships that were considered inappropriate or even criminal. For instance, adultery was a serious offense, punishable by law (Cantarella, 2002). If a husband caught his wife in the act of committing adultery, he was legally entitled to kill both her and her lover (Cantarella, 2002). In practice, however, most husbands chose to divorce their wives and seek financial compensation from the adulterer, rather than resorting to such extreme measures (Cantarella, 2002).

Incest was another sexual taboo in ancient Rome, with strict legal and social prohibitions against sexual relationships between close relatives (Cantarella, 2002). While there were occasional reports of incestuous relationships among the Roman elite, such as the alleged affair between the Emperor Caligula and his sister Drusilla, these instances were considered scandalous and were harshly condemned by Roman society (Barrett, 2002).

Homosexual relationships, particularly between adult men and freeborn male youths, were also subject to certain restrictions and taboos (Williams, 2010). As we explored earlier, attitudes towards homosexuality in ancient Rome were complex and multifaceted. While certain homosexual acts and relationships were accepted or tolerated, others were subject to restrictions and taboos.

Homosexual relationships between adult men and male youths were more restricted, particularly when both partners were of equal social standing. However, relationships between adult men and male slaves, prostitutes, or entertainers were more tolerated, though they were still considered to be of lower social status.

Roman society was more focused on the roles individuals played in sexual acts, rather than their sexual orientation as we understand it today. A Roman man who took on the "active" role in a sexual relationship with another man was generally considered to maintain his social status and masculinity. However, a freeborn Roman male who took on a "passive" role was often seen as compromising his social standing and honor.

Crossing Boundaries: Sexual Deviance and Roman Society

In addition to these legal and social prohibitions, there were also certain sexual practices and behaviors that were considered deviant or taboo in Roman society. For example, the Romans had a complex set of attitudes towards oral sex, viewing it as both titillating and repugnant (Richlin, 1992). While oral sex was occasionally depicted in Roman art and literature, it was typically associated with low-status individuals, such as slaves and prostitutes, and was often used as a form of humiliation or punishment (Richlin, 1992).

Another form of sexual deviance in ancient Rome was the practice of voyeurism, or the act of watching others engage in sexual activity (Clarke, 1998). Voyeurism was a popular theme in Roman erotic art and literature, often involving scenes of slaves or prostitutes being spied upon by their masters or patrons (Clarke, 1998). This fascination with voyeurism reveals the Romans' complex attitudes towards privacy and sexual desire, as well as their penchant for transgressing social and moral boundaries (Clarke, 1998).

SEXUAL TABOOS AND DEVIANCE: CROSSING THE LINE

Man performing cunnilingus on a reclining woman. Roman fresco from the Terme Suburbane (Suburban Baths) in Pompeii.

The Lure of the Forbidden: Scandalous Affairs and Seductive Stories

Despite the legal and social prohibitions surrounding certain sexual behaviors, the Romans were undeniably drawn to tales of sexual intrigue and scandal. Stories of illicit affairs, secret liaisons, and forbidden passions were a staple of Roman literature, providing titillating glimpses into the darker side of human desire (Richlin, 1992).

One such example is the tale of Messalina, the notoriously promiscuous wife of Emperor Claudius, who was rumored to have engaged in a series of scandalous affairs and orgies, even going so far as to compete with a prostitute in a contest to see who could sleep with the most men in a single night (Barrett, 2002). While the veracity of these stories is open to debate, the fact that they were widely circulated and discussed in Roman society reveals the enduring fascination with sexual deviance and the allure of the forbidden.

Sex, Magic, and the Supernatural: The Power of Taboo

Roman attitudes towards sexual taboos were further complicated by the belief in the power of magic and the supernatural. Sexual practices and relationships that were considered to be deviant or forbidden often held a certain mystique or allure, as they were believed to possess magical or supernatural properties (Graf, 1997).

For instance, the Romans believed that menstrual blood held potent magical powers and was capable of warding off evil spirits or curing various ailments (Graf, 1997). As a result, some Roman women were known to collect their menstrual blood and use it in love potions or magical rituals, despite the social taboos surrounding menstruation and the female body (Graf, 1997).

Similarly, the Romans held a deep fascination with the so-called "evil eye," a malevolent supernatural force that was believed to cause misfortune or harm to those who fell under its gaze (Graf, 1997). To protect themselves from the evil eye, the Romans would often use sexually explicit amulets or talismans, featuring images of phalluses or other erotic symbols, as a form of apotropaic magic to ward off evil spirits and bring good luck (Graf, 1997).

Exploring Sexual Taboos Through Art and Literature

Roman art and literature offer a unique window into the society's complex attitudes towards sexual taboos and deviance. Erotic frescoes, mosaics, and sculptures, as well as explicit poetry and prose, provide a glimpse into the various practices and relationships that were considered to be outside the bounds of social acceptability (Clarke, 1998).

For instance, the infamous "House of the Vettii" in Pompeii features a series of erotic frescoes depicting various sexual acts and scenarios, including some that were considered to be taboo or deviant, such as group sex and bestiality (Clarke,

A fresco in the suburban baths in Pompeii depicting sex between two males and two females.

1998). These images, which were intended to be both titillating and transgressive, reveal the Romans' fascination with the darker side of human desire, as well as their willingness to push the boundaries of social and moral convention (Clarke, 1998).

Similarly, the Roman poet Ovid, in his infamous work "The Art of Love," offers a wealth of advice and guidance on the subject of love and seduction, including some controversial suggestions on how to engage in illicit affairs or pursue forbidden relationships (Ovid, 2002). Ovid's playful and irreverent approach to sexual taboos and deviance offers a striking contrast to the more serious and somber tone of other Roman literature on the subject, reflecting the diverse and often contradictory attitudes towards sexuality that existed in Roman society (Ovid, 2002).

Conclusion: Sexual Taboos and Deviance in Roman Society

The intricate realm of sexual taboos and deviance in ancient Rome was influenced by a diverse array of legal, social, and cultural aspects. From the scandalous exploits of Roman emperors and their spouses to the enthralling pull of forbidden practices and relationships, the Romans' perspectives on sexual taboos unveiled a society both captivated and repulsed by the more hidden aspects of human desire.

Delving into the variety of taboos and deviant behaviors present in Roman society allows us to appreciate the wide-ranging and often contrasting views on sex and sexuality that existed in this ancient civilization. This exploration grants us insight into the intricate interplay of desires, apprehensions, and fantasies that shaped the lives and experiences of the men and women who inhabited this fascinating world.

References

Barrett, A. (2002). Agrippina: Sex, Power, and Politics in the Early Empire. Yale University Press.

Cantarella, E. (2002). Pandora's Daughters: The Role and Status of Women in Greek and Roman Antiquity. The Johns Hopkins University Press.

Clarke, J. R. (1998). Looking at Lovemaking: Constructions of Sexuality in Roman Art, 100 B.C. – A.D. 250. University of California Press.

Graf, F. (1997). Magic in the Ancient World. Harvard University Press.

Ovid. (2002). The Art of Love. Translated by James Michie. Modern Library.

Richlin, A. (1992). The Garden of Priapus: Sexuality and Aggression in Roman Humor. Oxford University Press.

Williams, C. A. (2010). Roman Homosexuality: Ideologies of Masculinity in Classical Antiquity. Oxford University Press.

The Role of Sex in Roman Politics: Scandals, Intrigue, and Power Plays

The Roman Empire, known for its grand architecture, military prowess, and enduring legacy, was also a hotbed of political intrigue and sexual scandals. For the ancient Romans, sex and politics were often inextricably linked, with high-profile affairs, betrayals, and power plays shaping the course of history. In this chapter, we will explore the role of sex in Roman politics, delving into some of the most infamous scandals and examining the ways in which sexual relationships were used as tools for power and control.

Julius Caesar: Affairs of State

Gaius Julius Caesar, the legendary Roman general and statesman, was no stranger to political intrigue and scandal.

His numerous love affairs, both within and outside of his marriages, were a source of much gossip and speculation in Roman society (Gruen, 2007). One of Caesar's most famous liaisons was with Cleopatra VII, the powerful and enigmatic queen of Egypt.

They met in 48 BCE when Caesar arrived in Egypt in pursuit of his rival Pompey. Their affair was as much a political alliance as it was a passionate romance (Gruen, 2007). Cleopatra sought Caesar's support in her bid for power against her brother and co-ruler, Ptolemy XIII, while Caesar was captivated by Cleopatra's beauty, intelligence, and wealth. Caesar's support played a crucial role in Cleopatra's rise to power, and she visited Rome a few times during Caesar's rule. The relationship between Caesar and Cleopatra produced a son, Caesarion, and cemented a powerful alliance between Rome and Egypt, with significant consequences for both empires.

Caesar's other affairs, such as his relationship with the married noblewoman Servilia, also played a role in Roman politics (Gruen, 2007). Servilia was the mother of Brutus, one of Caesar's most trusted allies and, later, one of his assassins. It has been speculated that Caesar's affair with Servilia may have influenced Brutus' decision to join the conspiracy against Caesar, though the true motivations behind this act of betrayal remain a subject of debate.

Augustus: The First Emperor's Double Standards

Augustus, the first Roman emperor, was known for his strict

moral code and efforts to reform Roman society. His laws on marriage and adultery were aimed at promoting family values and restoring the traditional Roman virtues of modesty and chastity (Suetonius, 2010). However, Augustus himself was not immune to scandal and accusations of hypocrisy.

While he publicly espoused the importance of marital fidelity, Augustus was rumored to have engaged in numerous extramarital affairs, including a long-term relationship with his wife Livia's sister-in-law, Terentia (Suetonius, 2010). His daughter, Julia, was also the subject of scandal, as she was accused of engaging in numerous adulterous affairs and was ultimately exiled by her father for her perceived immoral behavior (Suetonius, 2010).

The contrast between Augustus' public image as a moral reformer and his private life as a man who engaged in extramarital affairs highlights the complex relationship between sex and politics in ancient Rome. Even those who sought to promote traditional values and restore the moral fabric of society were not immune to the temptations and power dynamics that characterized the world of Roman politics.

Nero: A Reign of Debauchery and Despotism

Emperor Nero, one of Rome's most notorious rulers, is perhaps best known for his debauchery and despotic rule. Nero's reign was marked by a series of high-profile sexual scandals and abuses of power, which contributed to his ultimate downfall and the widespread discontent that characterized his rule (Champlin, 2005).

Nero's marriages and love affairs were a source of much controversy and outrage. His first marriage, to Octavia, the daughter of his predecessor Claudius, was a political union that quickly disintegrated due to Nero's infidelity and lack of interest in his wife (Champlin, 2005). Nero ultimately divorced Octavia and married his mistress, Poppaea Sabina, who was rumored to have conspired with Nero to orchestrate Octavia's execution on false charges of adultery (Champlin, 2005).

Nero's relationship with Poppaea was tumultuous and marked by allegations of abuse and violence, ultimately culminating in Poppaea's death, which was rumored to have been caused by Nero kicking her while she was pregnant (Champlin, 2005). Nero's third marriage, to a young boy named Sporus, whom he had castrated and dressed as a woman in a perverse imitation of his dead wife Poppaea, further fueled the outrage and disgust that surrounded his rule (Champlin, 2005).

These scandals, along with Nero's broader abuses of power and descent into tyranny, played a significant role in the erosion of his support and the eventual collapse of his rule. Nero's reign serves as a cautionary tale of the dangers of unchecked power and the consequences of allowing personal desires and passions to override the interests of the state and the well-being of its citizens.

Conclusion: Sex, Scandal, and the Fall of Empires

The role of sex in Roman politics is a complex and multifaceted one, with numerous examples of high-profile scandals, abuses of power, and political intrigue. From the passionate love affairs of Julius Caesar to the moral hypocrisy of Augustus and the debauchery of Nero, the intersection of sex and politics in ancient Rome offers a fascinating window into the lives and motivations of some of history's most powerful and influential figures.

While it is important to remember that many of these stories have been embellished or sensationalized over time, they nonetheless serve as a powerful reminder of the ways in which human desires and emotions can shape the course of history, and the importance of balancing personal passions with the needs and interests of the state.

Ultimately, the role of sex in Roman politics is a testament to the enduring power of love, desire, and human connection, as well as the darker side of human nature that can emerge when these forces are manipulated for personal gain or political advantage.

References

Champlin, E. (2005). Nero. Harvard University Press.

Gruen, E. S. (2007). Caesar: Life of a Colossus. Yale University Press.

Suetonius. (2010). The Twelve Caesars. Penguin Classics.

Medical Knowledge and Sexual Health: Contraception and Aphrodisiacs

The world of ancient Rome was one of both remarkable medical advancements and widespread superstition. The study of sexual health, contraception, and aphrodisiacs in this ancient civilization offers a fascinating glimpse into the complex and often contradictory beliefs and practices that shaped the lives of men and women in Roman society. In this chapter, we will delve into the world of Roman medical knowledge and sexual health, exploring the various methods of contraception and aphrodisiacs that were used at this time.

Contraception in Ancient Rome: Knowledge, Practices, and Beliefs

The Romans were surprisingly knowledgeable about contraception and employed a variety of methods to prevent unwanted pregnancies. While some of these methods were based on sound medical principles, others were rooted in superstition and folklore (Flemming, 2000).

One of the most well-documented methods of contraception in ancient Rome was the use of the silphium plant, a now-extinct plant that grew in the region of Cyrene in North Africa (Riddle, 1994). The Romans believed that the sap of the silphium plant had powerful contraceptive properties, and they would either drink it as a potion or apply it to the cervix as a barrier method (Riddle, 1994). Silphium was so highly valued that it was depicted on Cyrenian coins and became a major export for the region, eventually being harvested to extinction (Riddle, 1994).

Another common method of contraception in ancient Rome was the use of various herbal concoctions, many of which were based on the works of the Greek physician Dioscorides and the Roman physician Soranus (Flemming, 2000). These herbal remedies often included ingredients like pennyroyal, rue, and Queen Anne's lace, which are known to have abortifacient or contraceptive properties (Flemming, 2000). However, the efficacy of these remedies is difficult to ascertain, as the exact recipes and dosages have been lost to history (Flemming, 2000).

The Romans also made use of barrier methods, such as the use of vaginal pessaries made from wool, linen, or other materials soaked in a variety of substances, including olive oil, honey, or vinegar (Flemming, 2000). These pessaries were believed to function as both a physical barrier to prevent sperm from reaching the cervix and as a spermicide to kill any sperm that managed to bypass the barrier (Flemming, 2000).

Coitus interruptus, or withdrawal before ejaculation, was another method of contraception employed by the Romans (Flemming, 2000). While this method was certainly not foolproof, it was likely more effective than many of the other methods that were available at the time (Flemming, 2000).

Aphrodisiacs in Ancient Rome: Love Potions and Magical Elixirs

The Romans were not only concerned with preventing unwanted pregnancies but also with enhancing sexual desire and performance. Aphrodisiacs, substances believed to increase libido and sexual potency, were widely sought after and used in ancient Rome (King, 1998).

The Romans were firm believers in the power of aphrodisiacs, seeking to enhance their sexual experiences through the use of various foods, drinks, and potions (Dalby, 2003). Some of the most popular aphrodisiacs in Roman times included oysters, truffles, and honey, which were believed to increase desire and improve sexual performance (Totelin, 2009).

Wine, too, played a crucial role in Roman love-making. The

Romans believed that drinking wine in moderation could heighten the senses and stimulate passion (Grainger, 2005). Wine infused with exotic herbs and spices, such as satyrion and rocket, was thought to possess particularly potent aphrodisiac qualities (Dalby, 2003).

In addition to natural aphrodisiacs, the Romans also experimented with more esoteric love potions, often concocted by women who specialized in love magic (Flower, 2008). These potions contained various ingredients, such as herbs, animal parts, and even human remains, and were believed to invoke the powers of the gods to aid in matters of the heart (Betz, 1996).

Many of the aphrodisiacs used by the Romans were based on the concept of "sympathetic magic," the belief that substances resembling genitalia or other sexual symbols would possess aphrodisiac properties (King, 1998). For example, the Romans believed that the orchid, a flower whose name is derived from the Greek word for "testicle," would have potent aphrodisiac effects due to its suggestive shape (King, 1998).

Another popular aphrodisiac in ancient Rome was the sea hare, a type of marine mollusk that was believed to have powerful aphrodisiac properties when consumed (King, 1998). The sea hare's reputation as an aphrodisiac was likely due to its unique ability to secrete a purple ink when threatened, which was thought to resemble the act of ejaculation (King, 1998).

Some aphrodisiacs used by the Romans were rooted in actual medical properties, such as the use of the plant yohimbe, which contains a compound called yohimbine that has been shown to have some efficacy in treating erectile dysfunction (King, 1998). However, many of the other aphrodisiacs used by the Romans were likely little more than superstition and folklore, with little to no basis in actual medical science (King, 1998).

The Romans also believed in the power of love potions and magical spells to enhance sexual desire and attraction. These love potions, known as "philtres," often contained a variety of exotic and unusual ingredients, such as the ashes of a burnt swallow's heart, the blood of a bat, or the ground-up bones of a deceased lover (King, 1998). While these love potions were likely little more than elaborate placebos, they reveal the Romans' deep-seated belief in the power of magic and the supernatural to influence human desire and attraction (King, 1998).

Sexual Health and Well-Being: The Roman Approach

The Romans' interest in contraception and aphrodisiacs was part of a broader concern with sexual health and well-being. Roman physicians, such as Galen and Celsus, wrote extensively about the importance of sexual health and the role of diet, exercise, and other lifestyle factors in maintaining sexual vitality (Galen, 1991; Celsus, 1935).

For instance, Galen recommended a diet rich in foods like onions, garlic, and eggs to promote sexual health and virility, while Celsus advised engaging in regular exercise and avoiding excessive consumption of alcohol to maintain sexual potency

(Galen, 1991; Celsus, 1935). These recommendations reveal the Romans' awareness of the connection between overall health and sexual well-being, as well as their commitment to promoting sexual health as an essential aspect of a healthy and fulfilling life (Galen, 1991; Celsus, 1935).

Roman Medicine and Sexual Health: Continuity and Change

The study of medical knowledge and sexual health in ancient Rome also offers an opportunity to examine the ways in which Roman medicine both inherited and transformed the medical traditions of earlier civilizations, such as Greece and Egypt (Nutton, 2004). For example, the Roman physician Galen, who was born in the Greek city of Pergamum, was heavily influenced by the works of earlier Greek physicians, such as Hippocrates and Aristotle (Galen, 1991). At the same time, Galen also incorporated elements of Roman culture and society into his medical theories and practices, reflecting the unique synthesis of Greek and Roman ideas that characterized the Roman world (Galen, 1991).

Similarly, the Roman interest in contraception and aphrodisiacs can be traced back to earlier civilizations, such as ancient Egypt, which also had a rich tradition of herbal medicine and magical practices related to sexual health (Nunn, 2002). However, the Romans also added their own unique innovations and ideas to these earlier traditions, reflecting their distinctive approach to sexual health and well-being (Nutton, 2004).

This continuity and change in Roman medical knowledge and

sexual health is emblematic of the broader process of cultural exchange and adaptation that characterized the Roman world, as well as the enduring legacy of Roman medicine in the history of Western medicine and sexuality (Nutton, 2004).

Sexual Health in Roman Society: Public and Private Lives

The Romans' concern with sexual health was not limited to the private sphere but also had significant implications for public life and social relationships. For instance, the ability to conceive and bear children was an essential aspect of Roman marriage and family life, and the failure to do so could have serious social and legal consequences (Rawson, 2003). As a result, the knowledge and practice of contraception were not only matters of personal choice and preference but also crucial to the functioning of Roman society and the maintenance of social order (Rawson, 2003).

At the same time, the Romans' interest in aphrodisiacs and sexual performance also reveals a society that was deeply concerned with matters of love, desire, and attraction, both within and outside the confines of marriage and family life (King, 1998). The widespread use of love potions and magical spells, for instance, reflects the Romans' belief in the power of supernatural forces to shape human relationships and influence the course of romantic and sexual encounters (King, 1998).

In this way, the study of medical knowledge and sexual health in ancient Rome offers a unique perspective on the interplay between public and private life, revealing the ways in which the Romans navigated the complex web of social expectations, personal desires, and cultural norms that shaped their world.

Conclusion: Medical Knowledge and Sexual Health in Ancient Rome

The study of medical knowledge and sexual health in ancient Rome offers a fascinating insight into the complex and often contradictory beliefs and practices that shaped the lives of men and women in this ancient civilization. From the surprisingly advanced methods of contraception to the bizarre and exotic aphrodisiacs, the Romans' approach to sexual health reveals a society that was both deeply rooted in superstition and remarkably forward-thinking in its understanding of the importance of sexual well-being.

As we continue to explore the world of Roman medical knowledge and sexual health, we are reminded of the universal human desire to understand and control our own bodies and our passions, as well as the enduring fascination with the mysteries of love, desire, and attraction that continue to captivate us to this day.

References

Celsus, A. C. (1935). De Medicina. Translated by W. G. Spencer. Harvard University Press.

Dalby, A. (2003). Food in the Ancient World from A to Z. Routledge.

Galen. (1991). On the Usefulness of the Parts of the Body. Translated by Margaret Tallmadge May. Cornell University Press.

Flemming, R. (2000). Medicine and the Making of Roman Women: Gender, Nature, and Authority from Celsus to Galen. Oxford University Press.

Nunn, J. F. (2002). Ancient Egyptian Medicine. University of Oklahoma Press.

Nutton, V. (2004). Ancient Medicine. Routledge.

King, H. (1998). Hippocrates' Woman: Reading the Female Body in Ancient Greece. Routledge.

Riddle, J. M. (1994). Contraception and Abortion from the Ancient World to the Renaissance. Harvard University Press.

The Decline of Roman Morality: Sex and the Fall of Rome

The fall of the Roman Empire remains one of history's greatest enigmas, with numerous theories put forth to explain the decline and eventual collapse of this once-mighty civilization. Among the various explanations offered, one of the most enduring and controversial is the idea that the decline of Roman morality, particularly in the realm of sexual behavior, played a significant role in the empire's downfall. In this chapter, we will explore the intriguing relationship between sex, morality, and the fall of Rome. We will be transported to the final days of the Roman Empire, as we delve into the decadence, debauchery, and moral decay that some believe led to its demise.

Morality and Society: The Roman Ideal

To understand the alleged decline of Roman morality, it is essential first to examine the ideals and values that shaped Roman society. The Romans placed great importance on virtues such as pietas (duty), fides (loyalty), and gravitas (seriousness) (Cicero, 44 BCE). These virtues were seen as the bedrock of Roman society, providing a moral framework that guided both individual behavior and public life.

In the realm of sexual behavior, the Romans valued modesty, self-control, and fidelity within marriage (Cicero, 44 BCE). Extramarital affairs, while not uncommon, were generally frowned upon, and the ideal Roman citizen was expected to adhere to a strict code of sexual ethics that prioritized family life and the continuation of the Roman bloodline (Cicero, 44 BCE).

Decadence and Debauchery: The Dark Side of Roman Sexuality

Despite these high-minded ideals, the Roman world was also characterized by a darker side of sexual excess and debauchery. As the empire grew and expanded, bringing with it vast wealth and cultural influence, Roman society became increasingly characterized by hedonism and a relentless pursuit of pleasure (Suetonius, 121 CE).

Some of the most notorious examples of Roman decadence can be found in the lives of the emperors, who often engaged in extravagant displays of sexual excess and debauchery. For example, the emperor Tiberius was said to have indulged in orgies and other depraved acts on his private island of Capri, while Nero and Caligula were notorious for their sexual escapades and brutal treatment of their wives and lovers (Suetonius, 121 CE).

But it was not only the emperors who engaged in such behavior. The Roman elite, too, often reveled in orgies, gluttony, and other forms of excess, as evidenced by the infamous "banquet of Trimalchio" described in the Roman novel Satyricon by Petronius (1st century CE). This debauched event, featuring lavish feasts and erotic entertainment, epitomizes the hedonistic lifestyle that many Romans aspired to.

The Decline of Roman Morality: Sex, Society, and the Fall of Rome

The moral decline of Rome, as evidenced by the rampant sexual excess and debauchery, has often been cited as a contributing factor to the fall of the Roman Empire. According to this theory, the erosion of traditional Roman virtues and the increasing decadence of Roman society undermined the very foundations of the empire , leading to its eventual collapse (Gibbon, 1776-1789). Proponents of this view argue that as Rome's moral fabric deteriorated, so too did the discipline and cohesion of its military, the efficiency of its bureaucracy, and the loyalty of its citizens, all of which contributed to the empire's decline and fall (Gibbon, 1776-1789).

One of the most famous proponents of this theory was the 18th-century historian Edward Gibbon, who, in his monumental work, "The History of the Decline and Fall of the Roman Empire," argued that the moral decay of Rome was a primary factor in its collapse (Gibbon, 1776-1789). Gibbon believed that the decline of Roman morality was evident in the increasingly licentious behavior of the emperors and the elite, as well as in the widespread acceptance of sexual excess and debauchery among the general populace (Gibbon, 1776-1789).

However, it is important to note that this view has been challenged by many modern historians, who argue that the decline of Roman morality was only one of many factors that contributed to the fall of the empire (Heather, 2005). For example, the historian Peter Heather has argued that the primary cause of Rome's collapse was the pressure exerted by barbarian invasions and migrations, rather than any internal moral decay (Heather, 2005).

Additionally, some scholars have questioned the extent to which Roman society was truly characterized by sexual excess and debauchery, pointing out that much of the evidence for this alleged decline comes from the works of satirists and moralists, who may have exaggerated the extent of Roman decadence for rhetorical effect (Veyne, 1987). According to this view, the notion of a decline in Roman morality may be more a product of historical myth and literary imagination than an accurate reflection of the reality of Roman society (Veyne, 1987).

Conclusion: Sex, Morality, and the Fall of Rome

The relationship between sex, morality, and the fall of Rome is a complex and controversial one, with historians and scholars continuing to debate the extent to which the decline of Roman morality contributed to the empire's collapse. While it is clear that the Roman world was characterized by a certain degree of sexual excess and debauchery, it is also evident that the Roman people held deeply ingrained values and ideals that governed their personal lives and public behavior.

Ultimately, the question of whether the decline of Roman morality led to the fall of Rome may be less important than the broader lessons we can learn from the study of Roman sexuality and its relationship to society. As we have explored the fascinating world of sex and morality in ancient Rome, we are reminded of the enduring power of human desire, the complex interplay between private passions and public life, and the delicate balance between pleasure and virtue that continues to shape our world today.

References

Cicero, M. T. (44 BCE). De Officiis. Translated by Walter Miller. Loeb Classical Library.

Gibbon, E. (1776-1789). The History of the Decline and Fall of the Roman Empire. Strahan & Cadell.

Heather, P. (2005). The Fall of the Roman Empire: A New History of Rome and the Barbarians. Oxford University Press.

Suetonius. (121 CE). The Lives of the Caesars. Translated by J. C. Rolfe. Loeb Classical Library.

Veyne, P. (1987). Roman Erotic Elegy: Love, Poetry, and the West. Translated by D. Pellauer. University of Chicago Press.

The Lasting Impact of Roman Sexuality on Western Culture

As we reach the end of our journey through the secret sex lives of the Romans, it is worth reflecting on the lasting impact of Roman sexuality on Western culture. From our exploration of marriage, adultery, and divorce to the role of sexuality in religion and power dynamics, we have seen that Roman society was deeply entwined with the intricacies of human desire and passion. In this final chapter, we will examine how the legacy of Roman sexuality continues to shape our understanding of love, desire, and intimacy in the modern world.

Roman Sexuality and the Foundations of Western Culture

The influence of Roman sexuality on Western culture is evident in many aspects of our contemporary society. The legal and social structures of marriage, for example, can be traced back to the Roman concept of matrimonium, which emphasized the importance of mutual consent and the joining of two families in a legally binding union (Treggiari, 1991). This notion of marriage as a partnership based on love and mutual respect has continued to shape our understanding of romantic relationships and family life, even as the specific legal and cultural details have evolved over time (Treggiari, 1991).

Similarly, the Roman approach to gender roles and expectations has left an indelible mark on Western culture. The Roman ideal of the virtuous wife and mother, who was expected to be chaste, modest, and devoted to her family, has persisted in various forms throughout the centuries, influencing our conceptions of femininity and the role of women in society (Flemming, 2000). At the same time, the Roman emphasis on masculinity and male authority has also shaped our understanding of gender dynamics, with the figure of the virile, dominant Roman male serving as a prototype for the ideal man in Western culture (Williams, 2010).

Roman Sexuality in Art and Literature

The influence of Roman sexuality can also be seen in the world of art and literature, where the themes and motifs of Roman eroticism continue to inspire and captivate modern audiences. The erotic frescoes and sculptures of Pompeii and Herculaneum, for example, have been the subject of much fascination and scholarly debate, offering a tantalizing glimpse into the sexual lives of the ancient Romans and their unique approach to love, desire, and beauty (Clarke, 2003).

In literature, the works of Roman poets such as Ovid, Catullus, and Propertius have left an indelible mark on the Western literary tradition, with their passionate verses and evocative descriptions of love and desire continuing to inspire poets and writers to this day (Knox, 1986). The influence of Roman erotic literature can be seen in the works of countless authors, from the love poetry of Petrarch and Shakespeare to the modern novels and films that explore the complex nature of human sexuality.

The Legacy of Roman Sexuality in Modern Society

The lasting impact of Roman sexuality on Western culture is not limited to the realms of law, art, and literature. In many ways, our modern approach to sexuality and relationships is deeply rooted in the Roman understanding of love, desire, and intimacy.

For example, the Roman appreciation for the beauty and eroticism of the human body has been carried forward into modern society, where the physical form continues to be celebrated and admired in art, fashion, and advertising (Clarke, 2003). The Romans' open and frank discussions of sexuality and their willingness to explore the complexities of human desire have also influenced contemporary attitudes towards sex, helping to create a more open and tolerant society in which diverse expressions of love and intimacy can be celebrated and embraced (Veyne, 1987).

At the same time, the Roman legacy of sexual excess and debauchery has also left its mark on Western culture, with the figure of the hedonistic Roman serving as a cautionary tale of the dangers of unbridled pleasure-seeking and moral decay (Gibbon, 1776-1789). This darker aspect of Roman sexuality serves as a reminder of the delicate balance between passion and virtue, and the importance of maintaining a moral compass even in the pursuit of pleasure.

Conclusion: Roman Sexuality and the Human Experience

As we conclude our exploration of the sex lives of the Romans, it becomes evident that the influence of Roman sexuality on Western culture is both profound and enduring. From our legal and social institutions to our artistic and literary traditions, the legacy of Roman sexuality is deeply woven into the fabric of our society, shaping our understanding of love, desire, and intimacy in ways that continue to resonate today.

Moreover, our journey through the world of Roman sexuality has also revealed the timeless and universal nature of the human experience. Despite the passage of centuries and the vast gulf that separates us from the ancient Romans, we can still recognize ourselves in their stories of love and passion, their struggles with fidelity and temptation, and their search for meaning and fulfillment in the realm of human desire.

By delving into the intimate lives of the Romans, we are reminded of our shared humanity and our common pursuit of love, connection, and understanding. The enduring power of love, desire, and intimacy transcends time and culture, ultimately uniting us in our quest for self-discovery and the forging of deep emotional bonds. As we continue to explore and evolve our understanding of human sexuality, we can draw upon the lessons of the past to navigate the complexities of our own experiences, fostering a deeper appreciation for the rich tapestry of love and desire that shapes our lives and our world.

References

Clarke, J. R. (2003). Roman Sex: 100 B.C. to A.D. 250. Harry N. Abrams.

Flemming, R. (2000). Quae Corpore Quaestum Facit: The Sexual Economy of Female Prostitution in the Roman Empire. Journal of Roman Studies, 90, 38-61.

Gibbon, E. (1776-1789). The History of the Decline and Fall of the Roman Empire. Strahan & Cadell.

Knox, P. E. (1986). Ovid's Metamorphoses and the Traditions of Augustan Poetry. Cambridge University Press.

Treggiari, S. (1991). Roman Marriage: Iusti Coniuges from the Time of Cicero to the Time of Ulpian. Clarendon Press.

Veyne, P. (1987). Roman Erotic Elegy: Love, Poetry, and the West. Translated by D. Pellauer. University of Chicago Press.

Williams, C. A. (2010). Roman Homosexuality: Ideologies of Masculinity in Classical Antiquity. Oxford University Press.

Index

A

Adultery 8, 43, 46, 47, 48, 49, 106, 116, 117, 135
Aphrodisiacs 65, 71, 73, 120, 122, 123, 124, 125, 126, 127
Aphrodite (Venus) 9, 22
Art, erotic 20, 62, 65, 66, 71, 91, 93, 95, 107

C

Capitoline Venus 22
Catullus 28, 29, 30, 32, 33, 58, 60, 77, 86, 93, 102, 137
Childhood 2, 67, 91, 95, 96, 104
Cleopatra VII 115
Contraception 2, 120, 121, 128
Courtship 93
Cupid 8, 22, 24, 31, 34, 35, 42, 65, 70, 71, 72, 74

D

Divorce 16, 43, 46, 48, 49, 106, 135

E

Education, sex 2, 64, 91, 92, 94, 95
Emperor Augustus 46, 101
Emperor Claudius 109

F

Family 10, 45, 46, 82, 91, 92, 98, 99, 100, 116, 126, 130, 136
Fertility 9, 21, 22, 24, 26, 62, 65, 69, 71, 72, 73, 74, 92, 94, 98
Frescoes 21, 22, 24, 26, 53, 58, 64, 77, 86, 93, 102, 110, 137
Friends and peers 91, 92, 95

G

Gender roles 97

H

Homosexuality 2, 11, 76, 77, 79, 80, 81, 84, 90, 96, 104, 113, 140
Horace 79, 86, 89, 90

I

Infidelity 46, 117

J

Julius Caesar 47, 79, 114, 118

L

Legal aspects of sexuality 8, 9, 12, 14, 15, 17, 44, 49, 55, 81, 82, 83, 88, 89, 106, 107, 109, 112, 126, 136, 138
Literature, erotic 6, 8, 13, 28, 31, 32, 37, 47, 48, 72, 76, 77, 86, 93, 94, 101, 102, 107, 109, 110, 112, 136, 137
Love 5, 8, 9, 11, 12, 18, 20, 22, 24, 26, 28, 29, 30, 31, 32, 34, 35, 36, 37, 38, 39, 40, 41, 42, 43, 44, 47, 48, 49, 56, 62, 65, 66, 69, 70, 71, 72, 74, 76, 77, 79, 81, 83, 86, 89, 91, 92, 94, 95, 102, 110, 112, 115, 117, 118, 122, 123, 124, 126, 127, 135, 136, 137, 138, 139

M

Marriage 2, 10, 43, 44, 49, 50, 51, 60, 99, 140
Messalina 109
Mosaics 22, 77, 86, 102, 110
Mythology 5, 7, 8, 9, 31, 32, 34, 38, 39, 65

O

Orgies 109, 131

P

Pederasty 2, 85, 86, 87, 88, 89
Poetry 28, 29, 30, 110, 137
Pompeii 21, 22, 24, 26, 27, 53, 54, 58, 59, 61, 63, 67, 86, 93, 108, 110, 111, 137
Prostitution 2, 12, 51, 52, 60, 140

R

Religion and sexuality 5, 7, 31, 65, 73, 74, 135
Roman emperors 47, 112
Roman law 5, 7, 8, 10, 17, 49, 81, 82, 88

S

Same-sex relationships 11, 17, 18, 46, 76, 79, 80, 81, 82, 83
Scandal 16, 46, 80, 118
Sculptures 77, 86, 102, 110, 137
Slavery and sexuality 10, 17
Social classes 10, 52
Statues 62
Stereotypes, gender 2, 97, 101, 102

T

Taboos 2, 105, 110, 112

W

Women's rights 44

Glossary

Adultery: A sexual relationship between a married person and someone who is not their spouse.

Aphrodite (Venus): Greek (Roman) goddess of love, beauty, and fertility.

Censorship: The suppression of information, ideas, or artistic expression considered offensive or harmful.

Contraception: Methods used to prevent pregnancy during sexual intercourse.

Cum manu: A type of Roman marriage in which the wife was legally transferred from her father's authority to her husband's.

Dextrarum iunctio: The joining of hands during a Roman wedding ceremony as a symbol of unity.

Eros (Cupid): Greek (Roman) god of love and desire, often depicted as a winged boy or young man.

Flammeum: A flame-colored veil worn by Roman brides during their wedding ceremony.

Fertility rituals: Religious ceremonies and practices aimed at promoting fertility and ensuring a successful harvest or the birth of healthy children.

Gender roles: Socially and culturally constructed expectations about the behavior, characteristics, and abilities of men and women.

Homosexuality: Sexual attraction to, or sexual relations with, individuals of the same sex.

Infidelity: Unfaithfulness in a committed relationship, typically involving sexual activity with someone other than one's partner.

Lex Iulia de adulteriis: A Roman law introduced by Emperor Augustus to control adultery and promote family values.

Marriage contract: A written agreement outlining the terms and conditions of a marriage, including any property or financial arrangements.

Pederasty: A sexual relationship between an adult man and an adolescent boy, commonly practiced in ancient Greece and Rome.

Pompeii: An ancient Roman city near modern Naples, Italy, which was buried under volcanic ash during the eruption of Mount Vesuvius in 79 AD.

Prostitution: The practice of engaging in sexual activity for payment.

Sacred prostitution: A religious practice involving sexual activity in the context of worship or ritual.

Same-sex relationships: Romantic or sexual relationships between individuals of the same sex.

Sine manu: A type of Roman marriage in which the wife remained under her father's authority, giving her more legal autonomy.

Social classes: A system of categorizing people based on factors such as wealth, occupation, and social standing.

Taboos: Social or cultural prohibitions against certain behaviors, practices, or ideas.

Venus de Milo: A famous Greek marble sculpture of Aphrodite, dating from the 2nd century BCE, discovered on the island of Milos and now housed in the Louvre Museum.

Dear Reader,

First and foremost, I would like to extend my heartfelt gratitude for taking the time to read "The Secret Sex Lives of the Romans." This book has been a labor of love, as I have spent countless hours researching, writing, and delving into the fascinating world of ancient Roman sexuality. My hope is that you have found the journey through the lives, desires, and passions of the Romans as intriguing and captivating as I have.

As an author, I am continuously striving to improve my craft, and the feedback of my readers is invaluable in this process. If you have enjoyed reading this book and found it insightful, informative, or thought-provoking, **I kindly ask that you consider leaving a review on the platform where you purchased the book.** Your review not only helps me understand what aspects of my work resonate with readers but also helps other potential readers discover the book and decide whether it might be of interest to them.

I am deeply grateful for your support and the time you have dedicated to exploring the secret sex lives of the Romans. I hope that this book has given you a richer understanding of the complexities of human sexuality and our shared human experiences across time and cultures. Should you have any questions, comments, or suggestions, please do not hesitate to reach out. I would be more than happy to hear your thoughts and engage in a dialogue about the fascinating world of Roman sexuality.

Once again, thank you for your time and support, and I hope that "The Secret Sex Lives of the Romans" has provided you with a glimpse into an extraordinary world that continues to captivate our imaginations.

Warmest regards,

Harper Galloway

Historian and Author of "The Secret Sex Lives of the Romans"